Dying to Make a Difference

Mary E. Matthiesen

To the light that shines within us all.

Introduction

I wrote this book for love – a taken-for-granted kind of love often glimpsed at the end of a visit or hug, yet somehow radically felt in a single conversation between my mother and me days before she died. The power of that love inspired me to make a difference. It led me on a path I could never have imagined, meeting others who, like me, believe we can all live and die well.

Life-changing moments, like these – the big ones – bring front and center what really matters. You know the ones I mean: a friend's diagnosis, a parent or a partner's death, or even (if your work is in care) the death of a patient. In an instant, your awareness can shift like a tectonic plate, shining a light on things you were doing (or not) that you thought were so very important – and that you now realize don't matter a toss.

If you're at all like me, somewhere inside you want to do something with this profound shift in awareness. You want to be different. Yet you know there is barely a space in our culture or our all-too-busy lives to think or talk about it. Before we know it, though the memories remain, we go back to life as usual. Until the next life-changing moment, when we think we'll do something about it, sometime... later.

I can relate. This is my story, warts and all. A story about what death has taught me about love, letting go, and even leaving a legacy. A story about the power we each hold to learn from our experience. To make a difference. To change the course of our future and even create a culture of living and dying well. It's what these moments inspire and continue to teach me.

After my mother died, I was dying to make a difference. Not, as you might think, because things went wrong, but because they went right. I knew our shared experience wasn't the norm for most people, yet it was what 80% of the public say they also want for their future care: to have her voice heard and her wishes respected. To live her last days at home. To have told those she loved that she loved them. To consciously choose, after a lifetime of looking at the Serenity Prayer on her wall, to accept death and to let go. As her Baby Boomer daughter, I now knew why. Her death was one of the most profound experiences of my life.

I've spoken to literally thousands of people internationally about this conversation, about death in workshops, conferences, and, unexpectedly, over dinner when a stranger asks, "So what do you do?" Every time I'm speaking with someone who has their own story (and we all do), every time I'm with a group, there's a moment when we each recognize that we're facing our mortality. And every time that happens, we collectively know we are in this together, this life and death thing, and we want to make a difference. We want to make it count. We want to make it better.

What I know now is that we can. We don't need to reinvent the wheel, but we might need to bend it. To connect up what's already there, from the wisdom of our experience to the skills and services and strengths in our communities. I now know we can each start with ourselves, where we live.

I know this now because of what death has taught me about living and dying well. And what life continues to teach me: that we are each here to make a difference that only we are uniquely equipped to make. Yet to do so we need to have the courage, the power, and the freedom to choose. I now believe that facing death, not denying it, can offer us these three things, if we choose to accept them.

My mother's death taught me these things over the last ten days of her life. The lessons have been working me ever since, changing my life, taking me to places I never imagined. I'm far from done. I'm less than perfect. And I'm making a difference anyway, in the small and large ways that I can.

If somewhere inside, you're dying to make a difference in your life, with your family or in your community, yet you haven't found your way yet, I want you to know you are not alone. If you're still searching, I want you to know you count and you can make a difference, too, starting right where you are.

Right now. I don't want you to have to wait till death knocks at your door to learn what I've learned. If you're like me, I know somewhere inside you're dying to.

We are each our own experts; life and death are our greatest teachers. My story and the lessons I've learned along the way are not prescriptions. Every person and circumstance is unique. Yet I hope if you're reading this, you'll recall and follow your own memories, your own wisdom, your own inner nudge to "get on with it."

I hope reading our story helps give you courage to transform some of the fear or regret you may be living with and inspires you to remember the wisdom from your stories of the death of a loved one. To honor what matters. To learn from regrets. To choose freedom.

The greatest surprise to me in seeing my mother face death was the freedom to choose to live my life defined by what matters most to me, now knowing that I, too, will one day die. Life and death are profoundly connected, and each helps pave the way to the other.

My wish is that you find this freedom, so you too can choose to make the difference that you uniquely are here to make – in your life and the lives of others. You may find, like I have, that you are the one who can make the difference you've been waiting for all along.

What I've come to know, as a result of applying the lessons I've learned along the way, has become a barometer for my life, for living what matters most.

It's also become a vision of what's possible from that place, to create a better future for us all.

Within these pages, you may simply read a story about someone who wanted to make a difference. Or perhaps you'll notice places you might begin to make a difference in your life, in your family, or in your community, as a result of your experiences. I deeply hope so.

I can only speak to you from my heart, my experience, and my hope for our future.

It's what I've been dying to do all along.

For me, it all started with a conversation.

TABLE OF CONTENTS

CHAPTER 1

The Conversation

"I have something to tell you that I don't think you're going to want to hear," my mother said.

I had no idea what she was going to say next.

October 14, 2004, was just an ordinary day, yet it will forever remain the day my mother and I had one of the most important conversations of our lives.

I had known my mother was coming to the end of her life, and I had been avoiding it. But on a daily basis, my mother, Ruth Elizabeth Matthiesen, was not dying. Yes, she, like many older people, had been living with a grocery list of chronic conditions for years: congestive heart failure – check; pacemaker – check; osteoarthritis – check; high blood pressure – check; low thyroid – check; one knee replacement – check. But she was not dying, she was still living, and living quite well, thank you, very much at home. For some years now, a one-room apartment at Silverdale Grove was where Harvey's wife of 52 years (and widow since he died five years earlier), Jean and Mary's mother, had meals in a dining room with others over 70 who, for one reason or another, could not – or no longer wanted to – live in their family homes. It was a far cry from our four-bedroom, Williamsburg-esque family house, filled with a wall-to-wall library of books, the best furniture my parents could afford, and "silver polished when guests arrived." The owners and neighbors were lovely, and it was down the street from my sister's house.

True to her generation, Mom was always concerned with what the neighbors would say and wore her signature red lipstick and Chanel No. 5 perfume practically to get out of bed. Her smile beamed, her laughter was infectious, and her hugs to friends and strangers alike were soul-felt. Yet the usual, sometimes superficial, lilt in her voice was missing today. Something had happened with her "one good knee" this week that made it more difficult to walk than usual. (We'd always known her greatest fear was that she would be wheelchair-bound, as her own mother was most of her life.)

But this wasn't the whole story. She had been struggling for a couple of years with how to live, when she really felt her time had come but her body was still keeping her going. She felt she had no options as she held her deep value for life and a belief in God's will. She was 82 years old and felt trapped, but had been afraid to say so. That day she said so, and more.

"I have something to tell you that I don't think you're going to want to hear," she said.

And the next words she spoke: "I don't want to struggle any more."

Her words pierced any distance between us, a truth spoken so clearly and simply that time stood still. That phrase caught my breath and heart simultaneously, as tears flowed down my cheeks without the usual barrier between my emotions and my capacity to express or hide them from her. After all the mixed-up emotions and experiences we'd shared as a mother and daughter over the years – struggle and guilt, love and obligation, fear, martyrdom, and, at times, emotional or physical distance – somehow, through it all, there was a deep and undeniable connection between my mother and me.

In that moment I, her 39-year-old daughter, felt the reality that I would lose her one day. In that precise moment, I knew how much I loved her. She was a human being, sitting before me, asking the most vulnerable question we may ever ask another human being: Will you let me go?

I thought I was prepared to talk with my mother about death and dying, and, in effect, I was. We'd had some of the medical talks. We'd done all of that. She had a "do not resuscitate" order attached with a magnet to her refrigerator door to make crystal clear to any emergency services that she didn't want painful attempts to force her already weary heart to pump again if it did one day decide to stop. Enough was enough. But this was different. This wasn't a "discussion." It was a deep listening that opened the door to the question, "What could we do now?"

I thought I knew, as her daughter, what she wanted most: she wasn't asking for euthanasia or physician-assisted suicide. She didn't believe in them. She was asking me as her daughter, would or could I support her in letting go, whenever that was naturally going to happen?

Remembering this now, with my own mother sitting before me, I let go completely of the mental, psychological, and even analytical perspective of someone wanting to know her "end of life wishes" and dropped like a plumb-line straight into my heart.

"I have something I want to say to you, too," I said. The conversation was now leading us, requiring us, both to say things unspoken, to connect. Neither of us knew where the next phrase could lead. "I want you to be able to let go. I've been afraid if I said so, you'd think I wanted you gone. I'd miss you terribly, but I've seen the pain you're in, the struggle, and I know how angry you've been. I'd be angry, too. I don't want that for you."

She was all ears. "If you want to fight this knee thing with everything possible, we will fight with you, bringing everything medicine has to offer to support you. If you want to stop fighting, to surrender and let go, we'll bring everything medicine has to offer to support you along the way in that choice, too. There are pain medications and palliative and hospice care. Either way, we'll be your team, but you have to let us know what you want."

The tension in her brow and shoulders relaxed as her entire demeanor shifted. She smiled as if an inner secret had just found space to breathe.

I breathed my own sigh of relief that what I'd said in this moment was received with the love intended. I leaned closer, bridging the gap between the floral chintz sofa and the burgundy faux leather wingback recliner that, I must admit, had begun to look ominously throne-like around her frame, which had grown much smaller over the years.

After a moment's silence, while we digested the words we'd just spoken, she practically blurted out, "I guess I've been coming to the end of my life, but I've been avoiding it," almost surprising herself by her words.

"Me too," I said, caught completely in the irony of it all. "Isn't that just like us? It wasn't on the list, in the diary or calendar, so we didn't talk about it." We both burst out laughing, our cheeks full of the smile that told everyone who knew us that we were related.

As the realization of her life ending began to sink in between the layers of my denial of this obvious fact, I was flooded with memories of friends who had died, of speaking with my father before – and, as odd as it might sound, after he'd died – of countless stories of others who'd experienced the same. I even recalled times talking with my mother of her experiences since my father's death, as if he were still there with her when she woke. But, real or imagined, I'd never thought of these experiences in advance of someone dying, and felt the comfort it brought me to talk about this with her now, not later.

"And you know," I added, "I believe you'd still be with me even when your body is no longer here. You dream of Dad and have conversations with him." She'd told me of her very vivid dreams of him, where upon waking she was shocked to find he wasn't lying next to her. "Our conversations will continue," I said. "In fact, you may just be harder to get rid of when you're not limited by your body!" She laughed. "We'll always be connected in our hearts, and we both know that," I said, not really knowing where the words were coming from, yet knowing I believed them more than I'd ever realized.

A smile grew across her eyes and lips. As it did, I could see a peace take over her, as she became more and more beautiful before my eyes. Her crippling, deteriorating body and her fears of what was unspoken now no longer defined her for either one of us. The beauty of who she was, her essence, shone forth. I had seen this before with the dying, but never with the living.

I told her how incredibly beautiful she was in that moment. Looking back, I don't think I'd ever said that to my mother. Somehow we were intimately linked, and time stood still as this conversation unfolded. She almost glowed.

Then, silent tears streaming down my face, I leaned forward to rest on the arm of her chair, reached across to cup her face gently in my hands and in a slow, soft, deep voice, whispered, "You brought me into this world, and I will help you leave. I will do anything in my power to support you."

Without a moment's hesitation, she looked me straight in the eye and said, "You just did."

In hindsight, when I spoke those words in that moment, I didn't consciously know what I meant. It was as if the words just flowed out of me. I knew there must be a way to honor what she wanted for her last days. And we both knew she understood.

I sat back in my seat. We were both speechless.

This wasn't the first time my mother and I had talked about death and dying. She had lived through the deaths of her sister, her brother, her husband, and now countless friends and neighbors over the years. Yet every time my sister and I tried to talk to her about what she'd want for her care, her dying, the conversation would get so far and then she'd put up her hand, click her tongue, and say, "It's God's will, not mine." Shorthand for: "Enough, Mary. Don't go any further." Yet this time her hand didn't go up.

This time she was ready for more. This time, after our conversation, she knew she had some choices. This time she had questions about pain, about healthcare, about her belief in God's will. Fortunately, I had some of the answers, and I knew where to go for more.

I knew one of Mom's greatest concerns was that the timing for the end of her life was "God's will, not hers." We spoke of the God she believed in now, one who loved her and supported what was ultimately in her best interest. A far cry, to be sure, from the fire and brimstone God of her childhood, but Mom and I had discussed what held meaning and purpose and spirit in our lives over the years. The one she came to believe in after years of her life's lessons, learnings, and personal interpretations was simultaneously universal and personal. Life experience had taught her that her higher power wouldn't ever make choices for her; she had to do that. But she hadn't quite integrated this belief with her mantra "God's will, not mine." Though she truly was at peace with her God, with her life coming to an end at some point, and with some form of a life after death, because her body was still "ticking," she continued to believe that God had other plans.

Yet now she realized that both God's will and her own choices were equally valid. And she certainly had choices to make. Pacemakers and medicine and surgeries were all great supports when she wanted to keep living, but what now? That was up to her, aligned with her belief in God. If she decided, deep inside, that it was her time, and if this choice was in her best interest (according to her belief), the God she believed in would support her.

This was her interpretation, her life experience, her personal belief. It was also the most clear yet profound conversation my mother and I had ever had about religion, spirituality, and brass-tacks personal faith. It made no difference what I believed in that moment. What mattered was helping her remember what she believed in, what she found strength in, what could hold her in ways I never could. And just a few moments of speaking, it helped my mother call on this faith, her belief that supported her in her life and could support her hopes for dying well. This was shared wisdom between a mother and a daughter, and it would change my life forever.

We spoke about the choices she had about her future care. Did she want another surgery? No. Would she want pain medication? Hell, yes (my words – Mom would never swear). Even if there were other treatments that could prolong her living, staying vertical, would she …? Nope. Nada. Done.

We then spoke about what she'd want to do if she did know this was "her time." If she was preparing to die, whenever that time may come, what was important to her to do now? Who did she want to see? What did she want to make sure she'd said or done? She said very clearly that she'd simply want her family to know how much she loved them.

After more silence, it seemed she wanted to be left alone. Sitting across from her in silence, it was as if another world or depth had just been revealed to her, and it was no longer time to speak. We'd covered a lot of ground, both of us, ground that she had invited me in to share with her. Yet I was now intruding on what was obviously something deeply internal, intimate, and personal. Though I was profoundly privileged to touch it, this space and time was hers alone.

I silently stood from the sofa, kissed her on the cheek, and whispered that I was going home now. As I passed her chair to set my empty mug on the counter, I noticed her "In case of emergency, do not attempt resuscitation" form attached with a magnet on the mini-fridge door in her kitchenette. I knew that what was on this sterile document was true for her, yet it couldn't touch the soulful conversation we'd just had.

I was aware of every softly placed footstep to the door, aware of the hushed sensation in the room. As I opened the brown laminate door into the faux oil painting–lined hallway of Silverdale Grove, I was aware of my feet touching the burgundy carpet and of the smells of slightly stale air mixed with the leftovers from a dining hall lunch. At the end of the hall, I pushed the heavy glass door open. As the warm rubber border unstuck itself from its seal, a gust of warm fresh air and bright sunshine blew me into the outside. It felt so alive … and a bit odd that the day was still moving on as if nothing significant had happened.

I glanced at my watch and realized I had only been with Mom for an hour. It felt as if lifetimes had passed.

As I started the car and turned out of the drive, I found myself turning right at the end of the road, not left. Before heading home to be alone again, the car instinctively headed to my sister's house down the road. I had to tell her, as best I could, what had just happened. I had no idea what my sister was doing or if she was home, but I knew I needed the connection. On my way I wondered, "How do I explain this?"

"You're not going to believe this one," I started telling her about my visit with our mom. When I was done, we were both left speechless, as my sister told me she'd had a dream the night before about seeing the back of a woman dancing. When the woman turned around, it was our mother.

She hadn't danced in years.

Chapter 2
Unexpected Choices

In the very early hours of the next morning, a volunteer fire siren wailed in the quiet, wine-country town of St. Sebastian, California. An emergency call button had been sounded, and paramedics were called to 212 Bishop Street. An 82-year-old Caucasian woman, 5'6", was found on the bathroom floor in a pool of blood and rushed to the local emergency room.

Mom had gotten up to go to the bathroom in the middle of the night, her one good knee had given way, and she'd fallen hard against the porcelain tub. My sister phoned me, as she'd done many times in our lives, and I rushed back up to meet my family there. Given the profound synchronicity of our conversation, we all wondered if "this was it." Yet in reality we had no idea what was in store; she'd just slipped and fallen. We'd been doing this emergency room salsa for years with both parents, and there was no reason to expect this time would be any different.

We waited for the full assessment from the doctor on call and, as we visited Mom's bedside, I could see the nurses shaking their heads, concerned for another elderly patient going through countless treatments or surgeries. Mom was still conscious but in pain. The doctor on call took us outside in the hall to give us her prognosis.

We were told her neck injuries would heal, but her knee needed surgery badly. However, her heart condition and her osteoarthritis were not positive for the outcome of any surgery. If her heart could take it, she had at best a fifty-fifty chance of ever walking again, but it would require specialists to review her x-rays and lab tests over the next couple of days to see if there were any other injuries and to learn what might be possible.

Our family knew that Mom had no motivation to work through the pain and healing process another surgery would entail, even if the outcome was positive. She was no longer interested in being a stoic fighter. Actually, those weren't words I'd ever have used to describe my mother, but somehow that's what seemed to be called for, time and time again, as age and illness set in.

After the doctor had spoken to us all around Mom's bedside, my sister and I asked if we could speak to him privately. We told him of our conversation the night before, not knowing how he would react. It was amazing; he was so incredibly relieved. He immediately told us that he wished more families would have these conversations, as it is almost impossible for physicians to suggest limiting treatments in modern-day hospital culture.

Although he didn't say it at the time, nor did I as a daughter truly acknowledge it then, Mom was dying – not in any "TV show" sort of way, but in the very real way that most of will one day die, after a process of aging, bodily changes, and some sort of illness or combination of conditions. At some point her body would not take another medical treatment or intervention. And now we all knew that, deep down in her heart, she didn't want another treatment even if it could.

We asked what was possible if she didn't want surgery. If she was to be bedridden and no longer wanted to struggle, then what? What if she knew she was ready to let go? How could the medicine and healthcare that had sustained her for years support her in coming to the end of her life?

Mom was still in a regular hospital room. Specialists for her heart and liver and her knee kept coming in, poking and prodding. After a few days, her family physician came in to talk with her. He, very fortunately, was also a trained palliative care specialist. As such, he was able to see the whole picture. It was if he were the architect for a house, who understands the design as well as the beauty, as opposed to the electrician, builder, or plumber (cardiologist, orthopedic doctor, or liver specialist), all of who come in and out to check on their own bits, unaware that the whole structure is coming down.

On a day-to-day basis, most specialists are called to focus on their specialty and to "fix it." That's what we want them to do. But in the case of the dying, we need them to shift gears; palliative care is the gear shifter.

After listening to the physician provide the options and outcomes of surgery – given the physical limitations of her heart after years of congestive heart failure, her bones frail with osteoarthritis, and knowing she didn't have the will to go through surgery or physical therapy – my mother put her hand to her heart and said, "I don't want that. I can't quite explain it, but I know in here that it is my time." She then added, speaking directly to the doctor, "I have something to tell you, but I'm afraid you'll be mad at me."

Mom had made doctors into gods her entire life. Their statement of illness or treatment was gospel, which added to her confusion when different specialists throughout her life gave multiple diagnoses or conflicting treatment options. Yet this time she spoke more clearly than I've ever heard her. Ruth was in charge now.

"I want to do whatever it takes to support my dying," she said. "I want to stop my medications."

As we stood around her bedside, my throat fell to my stomach as I heard her words. At the same time, I was in complete awe at what I was hearing. To see anyone, much less your own mother, state that they want to die and know you are a part of that moment in time – there are no words.

I will never forget what happened next. Her doctor looked at her with gentle eyes and very professionally proceeded to tell her what her options were. He affirmed that he understood and heard what she was asking for, and that he was not mad at her. On the contrary, he was there to support her as his patient. He went on to tell her that there were no cures for the chronic, degenerative illnesses she had been living with for years. The medicines she had been taking were prescribed as the best options medicine had to offer, but these options were always her choice to follow – or not.

If she believed it was her time, she could choose to stop taking her medications and allow her body to take its natural course. He could support her with pain medications and care to keep her as lucid as possible in the process of letting go. He then went through each medication she was taking, detailing what they did for her and what would happen to her body if she stopped them. The picture wasn't pretty by any means, but it was true to what happens when systems shut down and a body dies. Other medications could be given to keep her comfortable, yet they wouldn't make her better. He mentioned that one of the medications could help her remain lucid without prolonging her life. By continuing to take that one, if she chose, she could have more time with her family, which was her primary goal.

With each medication, each new piece of information, the doctor reinforced that it was her choice to continue or stop them. She could change her mind at any time. And there were no crystal balls here, no knowing with any precision what would happen when she ended her medications. In fact, some people got better when they stopped taking them.

At each moment of choice presented, my mother choose to stop medications and reject treatments that were available. I knew then, and still believe in hindsight, that it was not "God's will" that was keeping her alive beyond the life she wanted to live. Rather, it was her belief that she didn't have a choice. That belief and a pacemaker kept her hardening heart muscle pumping. Thyroid and blood pressure medications kept blood and hormones pumping, and diuretics and laxatives "kept her regular." Had this been an entirely unemotional, detached experience, my mother's body, in scientific terms, was "matter" that science was keeping "alive." Yes, she chose her legal right to discontinue futile treatments (treatments that all medical evidence stated would not cure her heart, thyroid, or osteoarthritis conditions). There are no cures.

After all of the information was presented and all decisions made, the doctor told Mom that if she stopped her medications, "evidence-based medicine" suggested it could take three weeks for her systems to shut down own their own.

While we reeled in shock at this information, my mother exclaimed, "Three weeks! That long!" Once she had made her choice and come to peace with it, she wanted it over. Yet through all the medical details, scientific knowledge, and descriptions of processes, it was clearer to me than ever that we are not machines. The mystery of our own physical, emotional, and spiritual timing and process is its own – in our dying, as in our birth and our living. It was also clear that the emotional journey of her choice – for her and for us – was just beginning. It is one thing to choose what we want; it's another entirely to live out that choice and to ensure we will be supported through that process.

Chapter 3

Coming Home

The following days were a tsunami of details. There were final medical evaluations to ensure everything that could be done would be done. Hospital staff, who were angels at times and directly challenging at others, were whizzing like busy bees while Mom navigated her own internal process of letting go. There were some staff members who clearly didn't know or understand why a woman who came in needing knee surgery after a fall was now stopping medications and being referred for hospice care.

Our family was going through some of the most profound moments of our lives in a room where staff sometimes chirped in like it was just another day. They didn't know better, but they should have. This wasn't a hospice unit; it was a general hospital floor. But people die there, too. Those hospital staff who were kind and silent, respectful, and peaceful, even loving, somehow – those were "Mom's favorites," and she said so. They treated her with profound acts of kindness. She was in one of the most significant processes of letting go in her life, though to most people walking by she looked like just another elderly woman in just another room on just another day.

Amidst visits to her, my sister and I were trying to find a place for Mom to go next. We knew she didn't want to die in a hospital. This was an "unexpected visit," from which she, under other circumstances, would have gone on to recover at home. A care home was an option; my father had gone to a local nursing home after a fall and surgery years before.

At the time, my mother didn't have the strength to care for him, and neither my sister nor I had room in our houses or – as awful as it sounds – in our lives to care for him at home. We didn't think we had choices or options. We were able to arrange transport for him to come home for one short day visit, where he had his favorite scotch, his favorite food, and could be surrounded by the books in his library one last time before returning to a very isolated room. Days after, he stopped fighting and took his last breaths, surrounded by our family recounting memories, singing, telling him how much we loved him, and letting him know it was OK to go and be with those he kept "seeing" at the end of his bed.

Although it was traumatic up to the end, our family never knew which of the multiple "Kumbaya circles," as we irreverently came to call them, would be the last one at the care home. Yet even in that setting, having our family with him in his final moments was one of the most profound experiences of my life. Witnessing the peace that overtook him as he took his last breaths was like witnessing a kind of birth. Immediately after his final breath, it was as if the weather changed in the room, and I knew that although his body was still in front of us, he was gone. Many people have since told me sheepishly that the death of their parent, friend, or lover was "awful but beautiful, if that makes any sense." I can relate.

My parents, however, were very different people. The home my mother still lived in was a facility that required residents to be self-sufficient, so we couldn't build up her hope of going back there again. Nor could we predict when or what her last days would be like. At the same time, she couldn't stay in the hospital, and we didn't know if any of us could deal with going back to the care home where Dad died. Where could she go now? We had to do some research.

We re-visited the nursing home where Dad had died and were shown (clearly to the surprise – yet not exactly the shock – of the staff) a room with a disturbed resident sitting naked on the floor in the center of the room. The smell in the halls alone was enough to make us ill. And this was a "good" care home. Sitting across from the manager, who was reeling off specifics and handing us the admittance paperwork, my sister and I said we'd think about it (we had to keep our options open) and left not knowing what other choices there might be. In the car we were speechless.

My mother was a very refined woman, in her own way. She wore lipstick every day of her life. She was still fully conscious and processing the fact that she was actively dying. She was more loving than ever. There was no way in hell her daughters were going to allow her to live her last days in a so-called care home, but what other choice was there? Neither one of us had room at our home, and she needed care. We left the nursing home with the conviction that our mother would never go to a place like that and went to meet with the owners of the facility she lived in. We explained the situation to the owners, an amazing couple in a family-run agency. They sat with tears in their eyes, as they'd thought Ruth was coming home to live, not to die. But they said of course. If we could bring in the support she needed, they wanted her to be in the comfort of her own surroundings for her last days.

My sister and I cried all the way back to the hospital, tears of relief mixed with victory, shock, and disbelief at the odd dream that had claimed every moment of our lives since it began three days earlier.

When we got to her hospital room door, we looked at our mother. She had clearly been letting go of more and more things each day: the food she used to look forward to (Monday's blueberry Danish), or the event that she would go to (Wednesday night's live music), or the friends she saw that she was leaving behind. In the midst of this, she was dealing with the fact that she might never again see her bed, her home, and her friends who couldn't travel.

At that point, we simply asked her if she'd like to go home. Her eyes lit up. She said, "Oh yes!" And she began to cry.

My sister alerted the discharge service and hospice care. We told her doctor the news, and he arranged for an ambulance service to transport my mother home. The twenty-something-age paramedics were a bit perplexed as they moved my mother onto a gurney to go from the hospital bed to her home, and not the other way around, but they treated her with care, respect, and even humor.

Behind the scenes, my sister and I met with the local hospice staff and a home-care nursing service. We were incredibly fortunate to have some funds left from my father's insurance after his death to pay for some home nursing care for when the visiting hospice staff and volunteers would not be there.

Mom was thrilled to be coming home. To see her in her room in a new hospital bed – surrounded by her colors, her books, her furniture, her memories – was incredible after three days in a hospital unit with buzzers and shifts and constant interruptions. She met with her hospice care manager, was told about their visits and pain medication, and met with a home-nursing agency representative, all of whom came to her.

Mom, in her own way, was in heaven. She had caregivers who treated her like a princess, which, quite honestly, my sister and I couldn't have done. Our love and care were strong, yet we were unable to keep it up for 24 hours a day. After a lifetime of being with a mother who suffered one chronic illness after another, we were both still uncertain if all this was real. Whether it was emotional self-defense, or a history of caring for and about a woman who was prone to hypochondria, we both went into overdrive to handle the details and the emotions of the last three days before being with our mom "as usual." Was all this for real this time?

Chapter 4

The Call

Once the home evaluations were completed and all the caregivers were in place, my sister and I spoke with them about their findings. All agreed my mother was doing well coming off medications, and what we hung onto was that she would be in this phase for two to three weeks, as the doctor had said – or we heard.

She was lively and chatty and showed no signs of slowing down. She was eating and peeing, all her systems working as expected. There was no sign this was moving any faster. She was comfortable. She had care. And my sister and I both had been going non-stop since her fall, barely checking on anything in our own lives that might be happening outside this bubble.

My mother was constantly concerned that she was interrupting our lives. Although she loved the attention and being center stage, she didn't want to be a burden. My sister and I were both self-employed, which, thankfully, offered us the flexibility to drop most things when we needed to. Yet we had no one offering us sick days, and we needed to complete work for clients.

That weekend, I had a two-day business trip booked out of state. My sister and brother-in-law said to go ahead, as none of us really knew how long Mom's process would take. When I returned, I'd take over for them for a few days. I spoke to my mother about my work and impending trip. Looking back, when I told her I was thinking of going but was really torn, she said she'd miss me. Mom had never said that before. Although I heard her, I didn't truly listen.

I went downstairs to the gift shop and bought her a stuffed tiger (my nickname), to remind her I would be thinking of her until I returned. I went away believing that she had weeks to live.

I know what you're thinking. And, yes, when I first heard her doctor say "three weeks," I thought I'd be with during her every second she had left. Yet we'd had some 30 years of stopping our lives for real or imagined guilt-inducing crises: the last meal, the last visit, the last ... anything. Both my parents had been chronically ill much of my life, and this time, of all times, I decided to go.

Just for a few days.

The night before I left, as I was drifting off to sleep, a jet flew over my apartment. I remember to this day the surge of its engines against the silence. In hindsight, I realized that I flew all the time, yet I'd never really contemplated "leaving" before.

The alarm woke me from a deep sleep, and I grabbed my presentation and suitcase and drove to the airport. My colleague who met me there (and knew all that was going on) asked if I'd be OK if anything happened to Mom while I was away. I told him I didn't think anything would happen, but that it was OK if it did because we were "clear." She knew how much I loved her, and I knew how much she loved me. But that wasn't going to happen, because I'd be back in three days.

I spoke to my mother each day on the phone. We talked about how hard it was to be away from each other, but maybe it was a way of preparing our hearts to be apart, yet still knowing we were there for each other. She asked when I'd be home, and I said I'd see her the next day. She told me to drive carefully, and I had to explain again that I was in another state and had to get a flight.

I told her I loved her, and I'd see her when I got home. She said she loved me too and to drive carefully... again. Her mind was going, but I wasn't sure if it was the medication. Still, I believed I had time.

On the second day of the training, my sister called and said that Mom wasn't doing well, and I should try to get home. They didn't know how long she had.

I left the group immediately, went out into the hall, and got on the phone to the airlines. But I couldn't for the life of me get a flight out. I tried every airline possible, and all but one had flown their last flight out of the area until morning. A connection was possible, but they couldn't confirm seats to get me home sooner than my original ticket the next night.

When I finally got a manager to call me back on the phone and explained the situation, I was asked which hospital my mother was in. When I said she was at home, the airline said, after a pause of disbelief, that there was nothing they could do. The next flight was in the morning. (It was only after the fact that it dawned on me that they didn't believe it was urgent if Mom was still at home.)

I collected my things and walked up and down the streets from the hotel with my colleague, trying to somehow to hasten time. I tried to eat something, I packed my bags, and I went straight to bed.

The hotel room phone startled me from a dream at 5:00 a.m. (3:00 a.m. California time). It was a wrong number. I hazily remembered a dream I was having that my mother came to me, quite powerfully. She was as a younger woman wearing a suit, smiling. She said to me clearly, "You'll do it, what I couldn't do. Live your life. I love you." And she flew off. I rolled over and went back to sleep, and my cell phone rang one hour later. It was my sister. My mother died at 3:00 a.m. California time. We sobbed together. I can't remember what I said, other than I'd be home as soon as I could.

I remember eventually turning off my cell phone, which felt glued to my hand, and I wouldn't let go. Shock. Disbelief. Realizing where I was. I was numb and alone in a hotel room. In tears and with cell phone still in hand, I wandered barefoot through the hotel halls, waiting for elevators, weaving down more halls. I pounded on my colleague's door (it was 5:00 a.m.), said "Mom died," and collapsed into his arms in a puddle of slobbering tears, shaking with pounding adult grief.

Although it was in so many ways expected, I truly had no emotional preparation for what this would feel like and falsely thought that all we'd done and said would prepare me. Through my pain and loss and the millions of thoughts I had racing through my mind, after finally catching a hint of my breath, I was struck with another thought that nearly silenced the rest:

She did it. She really did it.

My mother had wanted to die. She was ready. And she wanted to be at home, her home. Somehow, we made that possible for and with her. She got what she wanted, what thousands would prefer, and what I myself would now choose. Despite all of this, I was still stunned. I just didn't believe it would happen as quickly as it did. I replayed what had happened again and again in my mind. I was as ecstatic for her as I was devastated for myself.

The last ten days I'd seen my mother in a brand-new light. In fact, in the past I had often wondered where I came from, as I'd been so outspoken but had never seen my mother really stand up for herself. But in her dying, my mother found her voice in a way I had never witnessed before. I saw her consciously and actively align what she knew and believed in her heart and soul – what she wanted and needed most – with her actions, her choices, and her communication. She spent her final days with loved ones, exactly as she'd wanted.

I learned through her dying that if she, of all people, could summon this courage – the courage to choose what mattered most, to speak her mind, to live more fully even in the face of death – so could I. I did not want to wait any longer to live my life with that power as well. It was, ironically, a power only granted to her by death.

Unexpectedly, my mother's death inspired in me the unconscious pursuit of one question: what was possible in my life if I no longer waited to speak what was in my heart? If I aligned my actions and courage with all I knew and believed in?

I took time to realize that I, too, had made a choice about the business trip, one I would live with and need to accept. I'd followed my head and not my heart. I'd heard, but I had not listened. This wasn't the first time, and it may well not be the last. But it was a significant lesson for me, one that has taken some years to come to terms with. It was a choice. I made it. My lesson. I knew, now, in no uncertain terms, that however long it is, life is simply too short to put off what matters most.

I wasn't with my mother at the end, but she wasn't alone. She took her last breath in the middle of the night with a paid caregiver beside her. I never imagined this would be the case. I was there with my father in the end, and somehow I thought I would be there with my mother, as well. What I now knew from lived experience was that if we want to spend our last days of living on our own terms, we will all need to be there with and for each other: sisters and daughters, but also healthcare professionals and volunteers– "strangers" who might be with us at one of the most profound moments of our lives.

Neither my mother nor I knew what path we were on when we had that fateful conversation. But pieces of it were already starting to become clear. On the long plane ride home, through streaming tears and (as one friend of mine says) "snot bubbles,"

I pulled out my laptop. To this day, I don't know how I did it, but it was as if all the work I'd ever done professionally and personally suddenly took shape on the page.

Chapter 5

Making Sense of It All

To this day I would like to thank the poor woman sitting beside me on that plane ride home. I was not just teary. I was sobbing, and typing like a maniac on my laptop, taking occasional longing looks at the clouds out the small oval window. When it was uncomfortably clear that I had run out of tissues, she gently handed me one. It was then I noticed I wasn't alone on that plane in my own bubble. When our eyes met, I knew I had to say something to explain this odd scene. I couldn't actually speak much, but found the words to say, "My mother just died, and I couldn't get a plane home in time." She looked at me lovingly, eyes glistening, and said, "Oh honey, I've been there," as she took my hand.

I had held the hand of women like the one sitting beside me on the plane before. Women asking how to talk to their parent or child. Women whose loved ones had died. Yet I had never been that woman myself. I had never sat in her seat.

I had seen death and dying from many perspectives, and I knew, more than most, that life was short. I had sat at the bedside of the dying, taught others to do the same, and I'd hoped to be with my mother as she crossed that threshold. I had seen it firsthand on the front lines with healthcare staff, with volunteers, and been at the bedside with my own father as he took his last slow breaths. So the fact that I was blindsided by my own mother's death was more than a tad shocking to me. The most shocking thing about my experience with my mother's death for me was that I knew all of this – in theory – before my mother died. The words now spewing forth on the screen on my laptop before me was an unedited dump of all of my experiences and emotions at that moment, in black and white.

You see, I had worked for 20-plus years educating healthcare staff, those who worked in sudden death and organ donation, and those who cared for the dying. I also taught volunteers how to sit at the bedside of the dying.

Yep. Me. The same person who was utterly shellshocked by her mother's death. The business trip I took, during what turned out to be her final days, was to teach compassionate care of the dying with healthcare staff.

Uh-huh.

I was a member of end-of-life coalitions, I sat on committee meetings with healthcare leaders working to raise awareness about advance care planning and end of life care. And I'd been one of the first in the country to work on organizational change initiatives within hospital systems in some of the most tragic

and emotional cases for the public and staff alike – sudden
death and organ donation. I had seen death in the ER, the ICU,
at nursing home bedsides, and in the morgue.

My work history prior to Mom's death didn't make sense to
anyone but me. It often felt like I was either living out some sort
of process of elimination or following an invisible yellow brick
road, like Dorothy in Oz. I knew I had gained a lot of the pieces
for some unknown something in the future. Each job, each role,
seemed somehow related to the next, but for some greater
purpose than the job itself.

So how do you grow up to work in death and dying, Mary?
It's a question I'm often asked.

You don't. Some paths find you.

I've always been curious, and most of the time I've followed
the very strategic plan written by my gut to the next – often
unforeseen – step. Though my background didn't appear
to serve me much during my mother's death, it did lay the
groundwork for what my mad typing hands were weaving
together on the plane.

The Head
Straight out of college I worked as an editor with McGraw-Hill
Publishing, helping some passionate science professors make
the complicated invisible realities of science and human biology
come alive for college students.

The Heart

I had been an executive director of regional chapters of the American Heart Association. In addition to fundraising, I led the first women and heart disease awareness campaigns in our region, through the shared stories of local women.

The Hands

Following my work with the Heart Association, I was recruited to be the executive director of Community Impact, a "done in a day" volunteer agency mobilizing busy people in Silicon Valley to give a few hours (or a day) to make a huge collective difference to non-profits that were serving needs in their community.

The Soul

After I left Community Impact, I felt a gnawing sense that my work had something to do with death and dying but didn't know what. I wasn't a nurse or a doctor, I didn't have clinical expertise, yet this path somehow felt true to me. I did have my personal and professional experiences, however, and knew how to develop education and awareness projects and programs.

Within two weeks (thanks to friends sending me out-of-the-blue requests they had seen that "sounded oddly like me"), I was co-authoring the Sacred Dying Volunteer Vigiler training program (think midwifery for the dying); leading workshops for hospice and faith volunteers to sit at the bedside of the dying; and developing workshops for hospice and healthcare staff with the creators of an award-winning spoken-word and music CD called "Graceful Passages."

Last but not least: The System

Years before all of this, I'd been hired to be the first hospital services coordinator working on the front lines with hospital staff and communities in sudden death and organ donation in Northern California. As the first and only non-nurse on staff, I learned firsthand the professional impact and emotional challenges staff feel about the death of their patients, and I heard many stories of family members' love and care. I was in the rare position of hearing and seeing the gaps between the two worlds. Working with the Transplant Donor Network also reinforced, daily, that not one of the people who died a sudden death got up that morning thinking this would be their last day on earth.

I saw it. I taught it. But I wasn't heeding the call.

Though my role in each of the above was ultimately to influence culture, community, or system change, I learned quickly through these various jobs that the keys to that change lay in three things:

What's possible:
People's vision, knowledge, or understanding of what's possible (the known facts, envisioned futures, possible choices, and achievable outcomes)

What's core:
People's beliefs and values, hopes, and dreams

What's true:
Not what people are told is true, but people's lived experiences, their stories

The greater the internal personal or group alignment among these three things, the greater the potential for change.

Until that moment, I also hadn't realized that from my professional experience, each piece, each program, each project was in its own separate universe, its own silo, its own odd stepping stone in Mary's work journey – and its own separate yet disconnected piece in my story, or any family's journey, to care for a loved one who is dying.

- Healthcare didn't know about the volunteer vigilers, and the two didn't speak. Community volunteerism didn't cross over to health issues.

- Education and training that was available for healthcare and hospice staff – about talking with patients and families, about planning for future care – wasn't available to the public, who were the ones caring for their loved ones and who most needed to know.

- And one other thing was missing. For lack of a better word, I'll call it the soul. Other than in personal conversations with intimate friends, or with those who'd also had "unusual" experiences during or after death at the bedside, the undefined world of "spiritual" experiences didn't seem to factor into any of this.

All of these had to come together for my mother to receive the care she wanted. And all of it had to come together for me, her daughter, to support her in having what she wanted in her last days of living.

As the weaving together of my professional experiences fell on to the page, there was a deeper level of personal questioning for me as well. I was a Baby Boomer woman living in Northern California. I had read dozens (probably even thousands?) of self-help books and been exposed to many religious and spiritual traditions. Although spirituality was significant to me outside of my work, and although chaplaincy was regarded as important to patients and families, "faith" wasn't a topic that was openly addressed in my work with healthcare staff.

At that time, I had the sense of "armoring up" in order to not only survive but to be taken seriously amongst care professionals. And though I wasn't conscious of it, I found myself leaving the deeper part of myself at the door.

Following my work around sudden death (and, coincidentally, the concurrent death of my personal relationship), I must admit I hit bottom. I literally couldn't bring myself to care anymore. Something had died inside. I needed to refuel. My skills and knowledge were strong, but my spirit was exhausted. I took time and committed to my "Big S" self beyond my mind, explored interfaith traditions and practices, and studied life coaching, all in support of my own personal growth.

I recognized that somehow, despite how much I cared about the work I'd done along the way, I'd left a part of me behind each time I'd taken on a job in the caring professions. I'd walled off some aspect of myself that was key to being me. I felt like I'd lost or given away a piece of my soul. And somehow I had to reclaim it.

Oddly enough, experiences I'd had around both parents' deaths made complete sense to my "Big S" spiritual self, but no sense whatsoever to my logical mind. And I saw no place in the "system speak" of work or healthcare to share what I'd experienced. Where do you put so many experiences of death and dying while you're living? Where had I put it?

Somehow, the seamless, unending keystrokes clicking away on my laptop on that flight home brought forth years of memories of families (my own and others'), experiences with staff and patients on the front lines in healthcare, connections between silos and services not seen before, eternally unanswerable questions on the mystery and timings of life and death, and powerful emotions between a mother and daughter.

Underneath it all was the reality of how shocking it was for me to realize that I, of all people, (insert your own image here of large, indignant woman with hands planted firmly on hips) with access to so much information and support around death and dying, who taught others, in fact, was still blindsided by my own mother's death.

I knew my collected experiences and skills were connected, but until I lived them with Mom's death, I hadn't realized all the gaps between what my head understood, what my heart was now left reeling with, and what I was called upon to be and do as her daughter.

As I sobbed on the plane ride back home, it was as if the puzzle pieces of my meandering work life slotted into place. The connections became clear between them:

- The information I as a daughter needed to support my mother;
- The conversations we and our family had to have to lead the way;
- The staff and systems that needed to come together;
- The community organizations and volunteers;
- And, through it all, the repeated and often unexpected experiences of listening and coming from the heart, which at key points allowed us all to support what mattered most and to have peace of mind – even when it meant bending the rules.

This happened when we didn't come from a fear of death, but were instead united by what mattered most in the last days of Mom's life, everyone understanding their role – great or small – in making that possible.

Connecting it up. From the heart.

I started to dream and envision. What if?

What was possible if the integration of all of this in communities where systems, staff, families, patients, and community organizations worked together to support someone's last wishes? What if there was no stigma around death and dying, but a coming together?

What if there wasn't a need to put our experiences away, out of sight?

As I asked these questions, I was blown away remembering the conversation that started it all, only ten days before.

I began to see connections on that plane ride back. Yet life had a few twists and turns in store for me before I had a clue what I could do about them. Because, as you well know, death doesn't hit the pause button on life.

Life… goes… on.

Chapter 6
Make a Difference?

The very weekend after my mother died, I facilitated a workshop for eight women and men courageously telling and performing stories about how suicide and mental illness had impacted their lives.

One week after my mother died, I was booked to facilitate a workshop for a hospital-based initiative around compassionate care of the dying.

And weeks thereafter, I was co-facilitating volunteers learning to sit at the bedside of those who were dying as part of Megory Anderson's work with the Sacred Dying volunteer vigiler training. As part of that training, I was role-playing a daughter at her dying mother's bedside.

Not an easy few weeks following my mother's death!

I remember thinking that I hadn't chosen to cancel a work commitment when my mother was dying, so how could I justify canceling these, now that she was gone? I, who had worked around death and dying for years, was suddenly on fire about the need to hear, tell, and share our stories – and learn from them. So, in a way, I was quite fortunate to have the opportunity to be with people who felt the same. I couldn't have expressed the profoundly life-changing experience I'd just had in "normal" society.

As I facilitated others sharing their stories, I wrote and shared my own. I didn't realize until I put pen to paper how little I'd heard of what I was now calling the process of "conscious dying" that my mother had unexpectedly chosen. My mother consciously chose her death; I was the one who wasn't prepared.

But not until I heard the devastating impact of suicide on mothers, siblings, and communities was the 180-degree difference between our experiences brought to light. The sense of trauma and helplessness still felt years after a suicide was the exact opposite of my family's sense of control, empowerment, and, though still grieving, release and peace of mind.

I shared our family's experience with a dear friend and colleague in a quiet moment while facilitating a retreat the following week. I remember summoning up the courage to ask her "as a professional" (knowing we both had aging parents whom we talked about when we saw each other) if my sister and I had done anything wrong.

Did choosing to support our mother in stopping medications or treatments make us somehow responsible for her death? Even though I knew in my heart it wasn't true, I still needed to hear it.

My colleague helped me see the simple fact that I was unable to before – one that existed before the conversation, before the choices. Mom was dying. Not in the "movie" sort of way, and without any big alert or crisis or sign to let us know, but she was dying. She courageously chose to accept this and let go consciously. She felt done and complete with her life, and medicine was falsely keeping her in a state that was no longer her choice. Had she intended to live longer, she might well have done so, even after the medications were stopped. We did nothing wrong by listening to and supporting what she wanted for her last days of living. Allowing my mother to die naturally was simply that – natural. It was love.

I realized Mom hadn't given up without hope; she had surrendered to what she knew in her heart and believed. She was given permission, in love, to let go. There is a world of difference.

It was then that I had my own "aha." I was aware of the gap that existed between my work world and my experience, the difference between all the committee meeting discussions and the focus on forms and advance care planning and why the need to plan ahead for our future care didn't reach the public. For systems, these conversations are about choices, forms, and a framework to deliver procedures and care. For families, they're about what matters most: love and letting go.

Working that weekend as part of a pilot project to launch spiritually based hospital initiatives to better care for the dying, my soul was uplifted, but my body was done. On the plane ride home from that final work commitment, I let go of all of the stress, emotion, and exhaustion of the prior weeks' events, and I became quite ill. I was diagnosed with bronchitis and pneumonia. When my doctor enquired if anything else was going on in my life, and I told him my mother had died, he asked, "Of what?" simply to note in my chart the cause of her death as a part of my medical history. Really lovely man. Clinically accurate diagnosis. Totally missed the point.

For me to recover I knew that in addition to medication, what I needed was time, deep rest, and healing. And a way to integrate all of the experiences I'd just revisited.

Once I was well enough to travel, I desperately wanted to write in my journal, which had been my therapy for years. I wanted to express and come to terms with all that I'd experienced and all that I was feeling. Recalling that long and delayed flight home after Mom died, I flashed on the memory that the connecting flight was coming in from Maui, Hawaii. I remember well seeing sun-bronzed families with matching straw hats and flip-flops coming off the same plane that I boarded on one of my darkest days.

Maui – where most went to tan, drink Mai Tais, and boogie board – had in the past been my own spiritual home, where I went to let my soul catch up with me. Now, after a lifetime of feeling consumed by responsibility to be there for my aging and often ill parents, I was an "adult orphan," simultaneously experiencing freedom and an utter sense of disorientation. I felt as if the planets in my solar system had realigned, and I was catapulted into a new place where, as one friend put it, there was no one between me and the sky anymore.

That was it. It was time to go back to Maui.

Two women in their eighties, whom I had met in Maui years before, had been inspirations to me. I called one and told her my story. It turned out she was going to travel, so her retreat-like home was free for me to use. "Come and write," she said. I knew this was my only break from work and felt I had to go.

I left just before Christmas, not knowing how it would feel being alone for this holiday. To my surprise, I was welcomed into a gathering of old friends for Christmas dinner, which I'd not at all expected, and afterwards I spent weeks alone writing, pouring out every thought, memory, and rambling from the ten days that had changed my life forever. I told others of my experience, and they told me theirs. And then they told me of others who had had profound experiences and would be willing to share as well.

I thought I was writing my own story, but these stories were working me. I knew there was something I wanted to do with all of them, something I wanted to share. Yet as I sat reading and writing the same things over and over again, I got fed up with my own capacity to contemplate my navel.

One day, feeling the pressure of something waiting to be birthed as a result of all I was experiencing, yet not understanding what, I did what any self-respecting woman in Maui would do: I took myself to the beach. And while sitting on the beach, I opened up my journal and wrote one simple question at the top of a blank page:

If I wasn't afraid, what would I do?

This is what I wrote in my red leather journal on the beach:

Create an international campaign to support proactive, conscious and humane choices for end of life care for individuals, organizations, communities and countries linked with the systems to carry them out.

Whoosh. It came out in one sentence without any thought or self-judgment, and this part even I would have trouble believing if I hadn't been there myself... I lifted my pen, sat back to take a breath and was stunned by the enormity of what I'd just written. With toes in the warm sand before me, the ocean only a few feet ahead, and water as far as I could see in either direction, directly in front of me a whale leapt and spiraled straight up out of the sea.

For once, in all the time since I'd arrived in Maui, I was wordless. And through all the fears and the doubts – the How?, the Who am I to...? and the How the hell? – and through all the indirect ways in which I've gone about it, this secret mission is what has propelled me ever since. Even when I get fed up and can't find the words to describe what it is I do or care about. Even when it takes an hour to express what someone else may be able to say in two sentences.

I struggled and stammered my way, with the help of more people than I can name in one book, into what came next. My mother's death was the impetus for the unplanned birth of one piece of that huge vision: Conversations for Life.

Chapter 7

Conversations for Life

So great. Now I had a big-ass vision. A heap of awareness. And pages and pages completed from my time writing. Where the heck do I begin?

It was 2005. I knew what it took for my family to achieve what my mother wanted for her last days. It started with the conversation. And I knew that conversation – and the conversations with her care team and community that followed – not only helped her get the quality of life she'd hoped for during her last days, it also was a conversation that I would live with forever, allowing me to have greater peace of mind now that she was gone. It was thanks to a dear friend that I discovered the name for my new idea. It wasn't conversations for death, it was Conversations for Life.

I also knew one of the problems with end-of-life information is that it has, until recently, been stuck at the end of life. We don't know what we need to know until we're leaning over what feels like a very slippery edge of a very high cliff.

Looking down, there is no safety net. How ridiculous! It feels as if you're the first person who ever needed this information, when in truth dozens, hundreds and hundreds of thousands of people, die every year... and many of those who've died have family members just like my sister and me, with stories about what worked.

I was an educator at heart. I had the stories, and I wanted to make sure I also had the facts. So after Mom died, I spent a year researching what people really needed to know to get what 80% of us say we want but only 20% achieve: to live our last days at home, if possible. I met with leaders in the field and read every book I could get my hands on. I applied everything I knew and had access to as a healthcare educator and started teaching people to have conversations that could make a difference for their friends and family, like I had with my mother.

At the same time, I knew it was easy to go to a great workshop, then step out into the "real world" where no one else was talking about this and feel quite comfortable reverting back into denial or silence. So I began developing plans for a campaign, led by the stories of real people, so these conversations could really make a difference for our future care.

Sure, there was a lot of information about advance care planning and living wills when I began, but nothing had really spoken to or inspired me, as a healthy Baby Boomer woman, to do anything about it. Looking back, I realized my sister and I, not our dying mother, were the ones who had needed this information. And what I now knew, in the depth of my soul and experiences, was that there was a lot of work to be done if we were to make this vision a reality for any who would want it. But it was undeniably, absolutely possible. If the power to choose a "natural death" were ever to become as normal as dying in a hospital had become, I knew I could do something to help make that happen.

Until my experiences with my mother, I didn't realize the connections between off-the-cuff conversations in the living room with my family; the options that existed in the community; the medical choices that would impact how or where Mom could live her last days; and all of the services, volunteers, friends, and family in her community that needed to come together to make what she wanted possible. But it was possible. And it was, over time, a series of experiences, conversations, contacts, and connections that enabled her vision for her last days to come together in the end.

I also had to come to terms with the fact that just knowing all of this didn't ensure I'd be the one to be there with her in the end. I wasn't there in the end with my mother. Someone else was. For her it was a part-time paid caregiver. For others it may be a volunteer. And for still others without family, community, or volunteers nearby, this choice won't exist unless we develop clear and workable pathways and systems to ensure that it does.

I don't have children. And even for those that do, their children may not have the time, personality, or patience to be the ones to care for them. In light of how geographically dispersed families are these days, this is very likely that most of us – including me – will want or need someone to be there with us in our last hours. But that person may well not need to be a trained professional – just a caring soul who knows how to be a comforting presence while nature takes it course at the end of life.

I realized the bottom line for me was this:

If there was any way to do something that might make it as easy in the future to live our last days at home as it currently is to end our lives in an institution, I wanted to give it a go.

So in 2006, with all of this awareness and a secret mission in my red leather journal from the beach, I set about to make a difference. I had done a lot of work in the past, and I had inherited my mother's secret gene for being able to find out anything with a phone call. Fortunately, I had two important means of access – my car and my telephone – to national leaders in hospice, palliative, and end-of-life care in the US.

This is what I did.

I found my voice and told my story.

I met and spoke with dozens of leaders, telling them about my experience and realization that the fundamental key to the care that my mother received was in our conversations with each other, with professionals, and with the community agencies and resources that existed. They were incredibly respectful and supportive, though I'm sure now that they wondered who the hell was this woman appearing out of nowhere with such a grand vision. In fact, a couple of them asked, "Who sent you?" (What was I to say, "Uh, my mother"?)

I did what I knew how to do best.

I was a healthcare educator. Based on the stories I'd been told by leaders and the general public alike, I developed and delivered a one-day workshop for Baby Boomers in my area in Northern California, to help them take the steps, as I had, to overcome the fear and denial of talking about what matters most in living and dying well, for themselves or their loved ones.

I kept the big vision in mind.

I continued to speak with leaders nationally about what I affectionately started calling the Big Kahuna (a Hawaiian term for a great and healing master): my version of an emerging plan for a public-led, community-driven, international awareness campaign that included film, website, and community-based workshops to raise awareness about the need for – and the benefits of – having these conversations now, for the living, for the dying, and for our future.

I continued to ask for support.

All was going well. Lots of things just fell into place. I wasn't always conscious of it at the time, but I was very connected to what I call "Big S and little s support." Here are two examples: When I realized I would tire of telling my mother's emotional story in the public workshops, yet believed the story was key, the very next day I was walking my dog and met a cameraman in the dog park who offered to film my story for free. As part of the Big Kahuna vision, I had a dream where one of the leaders in the human potential movement told me his story. Months later, when I shared my dream with this same dog-walking cameraman, he not only knew him, he offered to send him an introduction, which made the filming of his interview possible.

Doing these four things started me out and continued to help me begin to make a difference. The feedback for the first workshops was overwhelmingly positive:

"This is the missing piece."

"So much of this has been about laws or medicine, this conversation is about love."

The people I was meeting were inspired and inspiring. Articles about the workshops were published in local papers. Without realizing it, I was getting on with the dream... or perhaps the dream was getting on with me.

Yet life has its way of throwing curve balls, and throw it did. Amidst the grand plans and workshops, I fell smack-dab in love. Yep. The real deal. The open-hearted, don't-want-to-live-without-it kind of love. We'd met years before at a facilitator training where we wrote and performed our life stories. We'd earned a deep respect for the soft-hearted and the "jump into the fire" approaches to life shared intimately in that week-long process. We came from different countries and thought we'd stay in touch – possibly one day even work together.

Sure.

We stayed in touch, visited a few times, having long talks and walks and truth-telling about our deepest hopes and fears in life. Yet on this final visit, on the way to the airport, the true feelings between us were spoken. With one teensy-weensy problem. OK, two.

First, my love was a Brit, and I am an American. Second, we are both women. Just to clarify, nationality in and of itself is not a problem, and being two women is also not a problem. But try 3,000 miles apart and an eight-hour time difference for a starter definition of geographically undesirable. And then add that at that time – yes, 2006 – we couldn't legally stay together as a couple in the land of the free and the brave. Federal immigration wouldn't allow her to stay in the US without lying about our relationship or being sponsored by a company. And neither of us is the lying or the "company" type.

So after much wheel-spinning about what came next, where to live in this geographically undesirable relationship, and too many flights between countries in the days before Skype or iChat (the only limitations of both are touch), once again death paved the way for my decision making.

Life is short. Love is real. If I was lucky enough to share this feeling with another human being, what was stopping me? This time I wouldn't put my head above my heart. Love versus immigration, when it came down to it? Love won. I packed everything I owned (not much!) into storage, and two weeks later I moved to the UK to be with the love of my life – with absolutely no clue where life would take us or how this work or vision might continue on.

Picture this: I moved from the San Francisco Bay area, where there was an Apple Store and a Starbucks on practically every corner, to a village the size of a postage stamp where we didn't have a telephone line and you had to walk to the bridge at the end of the road by the pub on the corner to get an internet signal. Forgive me, dear neighbors in rural England, when I say that at first it was sort of like a long holiday in an episode of Mary Poppins, which the chimney pots on the slate roofed stone houses across the street reminded me of. (Actually, imagine their surprise having a Californian show up on their doorstep. We each sounded like a movie to each other.) Or more recently, learning the names of the streets and areas and literally feeling the age of the land beneath my feet in the land of stone circles and Celtic wisdom – it was hard not to think of Hogwarts.

After landing in England for what we thought was six months – "Things would change, and we could come back home" – I started to realize this wasn't a holiday. My partner, who'd also unexpectedly fallen in love with the US, had to re-start the business she'd left. I couldn't get a visa to work for a year-and-a-half and had long since run out of money. And after getting loads of interviews due to my understanding and experience in work related to death and dying from my past in the US, I learned quickly that my odd résumé didn't "tick the boxes" required to land a job in the UK.

One day, as I was typing yet another résumé to send off to some part of England I couldn't even find on a map, I saw a sign out my upstairs window that the local MP (Minister of Parliament), was in the village. I could see that outside the post office, down the street, were local ladies and gentleman – most in their 70s, grey-haired and woolen-coated with facial expressions only the Cumbrian weather can etch – waiting to share their opinion and concerns with the local politician.

I had no voting rights, no reason to be listened to, and truly still couldn't understand some of the accents or local subtleties of communication, but I had one thing in my favor. I had a vision and was passionate about putting my experience and skills to use. And I had enough pent-up frustration that gave me the courage to go out and stand in that "queue" myself.

It wasn't until I was in line that I thought, "What the hell will he think of this? What am I going to say? I don't really even know if he'll listen."

I heard others in front of me speak about their heating bill or not getting a letter back about a dispute. Or thanking him for following up on a local hospital need. Each only took three or four minutes. With each one, he made a note of their name to follow up. And then it was my turn.

"My name is Mary Matthiesen," I said. "I moved here from the US, and though I live here with my partner I can't vote for you yet. But I'm hoping you can help me. And I know there are a lot of elderly people here. I have delivered workshops to staff and the public about end-of-life conversations and care in the US and have plans for a public-awareness campaign – all based on my experience with my own mother's death and the conversations we had that made a difference. I figure this is your local area, and you know who's doing innovative work."

And he looked at me, paused and said, "This is an issue near and dear to my heart. I have my own personal story. And there are two people in the area you should meet. You can use my name. And tell me how it turns out. In a few months time, I

imagine you'll know more about what's happening here than
I do."

Bam!

I could hardly believe it. I asked. He answered. It all seemed
so bloody simple. At the time, I thought he was just being kind.
How could I know more than he? In hindsight, I realize he was
being honest.

I emailed the first contact: a hospice medical director in
a nearby town. We met and, after discovering that we "spoke
the same language," she wanted see what I could do. She had
medical students on rotation in her hospice and invited me to
present two sessions for them. From there, she recommended
my workshops for staff in the area. I'd done my research. And I
connected from my heart. The workshops were a success. They
helped me to re-gain my confidence. I will forever be grateful
for that open door.

I then gathered the courage to send the second email, to the
medical director and public health leader in the region, who
I'd learned was "an innovator." I was given an appointment and
told I'd have about 30 seconds. On my way there (still learning
how to drive on the wrong side of the road), I got lost on the
roundabouts (how do you turn right off a circle?), and nerves
were getting the better of me. As I saw the building, I took some
deep breaths and again thought (you'd think I'd learn by now,
but no), "What am I going to say to this man who doesn't know
me from Adam?"

And when he walked in the room, clearly between meetings, coat in hand (note: not putting it down to stay), he said, "So, what did you want to meet about?" And I said, "I want to change the world, and I've heard you're someone who can help me do it."

After I told him my story, he told me his. And he told me that he'd wanted to do something to forward end-of-life care as a public health director for 25 years. It had been part of his written aims years ago, and now was the time to reach the healthy public with the message about planning ahead for our future end-of-life care.

He'd witnessed and lived personally the impact death had on the living and also understood, as I had learned, that the Department of Health in the UK was just about to launch the first National End of Life Care Strategy in the world.

He'd worked on initiatives with Healthy Cities and the World Health Organization in the past. And knew that palliative care for all is one of the World Health Organization aims. After that five-minute meeting, he left me with his deputy director and said, "See if you think she can pull this off. If she can, set up another meeting." His deputy director had a Wonder Woman sticker on her door. Need I say more?

For once, the mix of everything I'd done in the past, combined with my Big Kahuna plan, had a landing pad. And the greatest miracle of all? Months later they found the funding to pilot a campaign.

So there I was, living in a foreign country, delivering workshops to healthcare staff, and taking on leading the first community-wide public health campaign to overcome the fears and taboo of talking about death and dying in the country where the hospice movement began.

My partner, though thrilled for me and the vision, thought I was a bit mad and feared a bit for my life that I would undertake something so big, especially when I didn't know much about how things worked here. All I can say is, I knew what I had to do. It didn't feel like courage at the time. It felt like living my life. It was my calling.

I quickly realized that although the American and British healthcare systems were radically different, the fears, denial, and hopes around our last days were the same:

- Talking about death and dying was as taboo a subject for the public in England as in America.
- Staff were expected to start conversations and lead processes with patients and families without addressing their own beliefs and fears.
- Community organizations existed, but they weren't connected in a way that made it easy for the public to learn where to go for information early or support over time.
- And everyone I met – professionals as well as the public – had their own stories.

Fast forward three years in the region where I now lived. We launched a mini-version of the Big Kahuna: the first proactive, community-wide public and professional awareness

Conversations for Life initiative, to break the taboo of talking about death and dying in order to have a say in our future care.

The campaign was based on the filmed stories of local people, with those stories serving as a jumping-off point for showing why this subject mattered in the real world. We were giving the public information about what was available in their own communities and showing them how to start their own conversations.

And do you know what? Their stories, the lived experiences of people in a region of 500,000 people, all accustomed to a national healthcare system thousands of miles from where I was raised and where my own mother died, echoed the exact same things that I'd heard in the US. People who have been there have stories to tell about why we need to do this differently. People listened. The public, staff, and communities listened. And they are still listening to those stories today.

The pilot project received a national endorsement by the Department of Health End of Life Care program in England, and just as the momentum was growing and the project steering group had defined next steps to roll this out to all staff and the public across the region, the project funding ended. It ended. We'd all hoped that success would translate to another year of funding. I, completely naively, couldn't imagine investing that much and then: nothing.

We were about to enter one of the greatest shake-ups in 60 years of NHS history. Everyone from senior mangers to frontline staff was uncertain about their jobs, and nothing, other than direct care of patients, was being "commissioned."

Death, which wasn't exactly a health priority before this, clearly wasn't a priority now. Following a great pilot, others got on with their jobs. Life as usual. For me, it was one of the worst years of my life. I couldn't believe we'd come this far, only to have it end up on a shelf. I just couldn't let go of the vision ... of the stories people told, of what we all wanted to see, about what I believed was possible, of the red leather journal on the beach in Maui.

Could communities raise awareness about end-of-life conversations and care? Could people work together, even on a small scale, to turn the fear and taboo of talking about death and dying into their own community-wide campaign for living and dying well? Absolutely they could. We'd started it. I'd just seen a glimpse of it in action.

Thank goodness a few others saw the possibilities, too. A colleague who I'd met early on in England was a hospice director. She'd been raised in Ireland, where communities naturally came together around life transitions, and had held a vision about engaging communities with the wisdom that hospices had to share. She knew of the work I was doing. She'd read my Big Kahuna plan. And she'd been working with her hospice and her board to further support the idea of engaging the public beyond the walls of the hospice. But she needed a simple way to begin, while I needed a way to engage communities beyond the top-down campaign method we'd just launched in Cumbria, given the realities of budgets and time.

I met with her small team, as I believed that the local hospice was positioned in the community to spread the word, through trust and contacts, with those they'd served over the years. Consulting with them, I developed an approach for the hospice to convene 30 community leaders and members to contribute to, develop, and launch their own community-wide awareness campaign. The events were a success. At one moment after the "asset-mapping" of strengths and skills in the room, I asked what was possible now. A regional commissioner stood up and stated, "If the walls came down between us, we could reach and care for everyone in our community."

I didn't need to say a word. The weight of that statement was palpable and visible in the room. Although budgets were tight and roles were changing, although forms and systems and community organizations would always be in flux, if the walls came down between all of the services and organizations in the room, if we brought the gifts, the strengths, the skills and experience combined with the commonality of what we truly hoped for our last days of living – there is no doubt that we could care for us all, mind, body and spirit.

Head, heart, hands, soul, and system.

It didn't hurt that I could share the film and the website from our first community-wide pilot. It didn't hurt that the players in the room represented both small grass-roots support groups as well as those holding the levers of power for system change. It didn't hurt that everyone in that room, no matter what their role, had a story. And that each and every one of them was also going to one day be the recipient of the care that was co-created from that day forward. Every single one.

That event was the catalyst for that community – and for a simple process to engage communities in end-of-life conversations and care, starting with the assets that already exist. Following those events, that community worked together to develop a collective proposal and received funding for a three-year staffed project. Three years in, this small project, with tremendous commitment, leadership, and passion, has embedded public engagement and palliative/hospice care as part of an integrated, region-wide Living and Dying Well initiative – one of the first in the country.

A year later, realizing the challenges faced by other communities following a fantastic national campaign in the UK (called Dying Matters, Let's Talk About It), healthcare staff in charge of leading local community events realized how many of the public weren't ready to "talk death" in supermarkets or wear the T-shirt for a one-week campaign. They needed something more than one day or week a year.

With this in mind, I received a call from a commissioner I knew who told me of their dilemma. When I told her about the community facilitation I'd developed, a light bulb in her head came on. Though neither of us knew at the outset if it would work across an entire region, representing both rural and inner-city communities, we both trusted that the people should lead the way.

Over six months we worked with local hospice and volunteer agencies to convene 30 of their local community organizations. Every one of them, in small and large ways, is now in process of leading their own initiatives. Every one of the people and the organizations represented had their own stories and their own reasons for wanting to make a difference. And every one of them will be the recipient of what they create in the communities where they live.

From bucket list campaigns to horse-drawn hearses in city centers; from funeral home staff visiting hospices to share how they could help families prepare for their future together, and vice versa; from volunteer peer educators leading free public workshops to managers who simply raised their voice at monthly meetings to ask where bereavement care fit on the organization's agenda; 30 people in six communities became 300, which became 3000, and more. Small steps create great ripples when people's hearts are united towards a common goal.

The work they have done is fantastic. Those communities that committed to forwarding this movement have worked in different ways, some in fits and starts. Others found the support of paid staff who'd never held such a role.

We are all forging new territory. I know it hasn't been easy. There is still much work to be done. Yet some of these communities are now shining examples in an international movement called Compassionate Communities – where compassionate care for the dying is viewed not as a medical event, but a social, spiritual, and community experience. And every community, large or small, that chooses to is building on and creating new opportunities for support, for connections, and for care that are creating a new future for us all.

What I now knew, as a transplanted American, was that the need for this sort of campaign for engaging communities was international (particularly in more Westernized countries). The belief that "my healthcare insurance" or "my system" or "my country/government" was the reason we weren't getting the care we wanted for our last days was bogus. This movement, this need to create compassionate community approaches to care for all our days, was international, not just in starting the conversation, but in creating connections across communities to care.

When I got on the phone to friends in the US, or visited and shared what we were doing, I had people ask how they could be part of it, how their community could have what we'd started doing in England. I was asked, "How are you able to use the D-word?" I learned quickly that many of those working in end-of-life care in the US had been effectively silenced by the "death panel" debacle, while we were working on public-awareness campaigns abroad. And I knew that the stories and the strengths that we'd begun to mobilize here existed abroad as well.

Chapter 8

Being the Change

I knew what was possible now. Excited to see the ripples of people making a difference, I was now leading sessions for staff and communities to start conversations and catalyze these connections. I was presenting outcomes of our work at international conferences. It struck a chord with key initiatives on advance care planning (medical term for planning ahead for your future care).

Yet inwardly, it started to feel like something key was missing. For me, it was again becoming about the doing, not the being. So I sat myself down again to ask myself if I was doing what I was here to do. And the answer, the "problem" that came to me that was causing my angst amidst all this seeming success, was this: even with all I knew and the conversations we'd had, nothing had really prepared me for my mother's death.

I was becoming better prepared for my future care and helping communities to do the same, but was I any more prepared for the fact that I would one day die?

The fact was, with all I knew about end-of-life care, I was incredibly unprepared for death: my mother's or my own.

I had been teaching others that life was short, and we needed to talk about and prepare for it, yet until my mother's death, I hadn't applied any of this to myself. I hadn't had "the conversation" for myself, hadn't explored what I'd want and what I'd choose.

Before I developed the first workshops for others to break the taboo, even though I knew the content, I had to own up to this. How could I possibly consider standing before others, as deep as my passion about this work was, without having done anything about it myself? My parents were gone. The love of my life, my sister, their families, and my circle of friends were now my family. Truly there was no one between me and the sky anymore. And I could no longer deny that one day I will die, too.

So before I could presume to speak to others, I had to do it myself. Inspired by my mother's courage and choices and the realization that I was next, I overcame my own denial and spent a weekend with my love having our own conversations.

We shared what we'd want for our own future care, including our last days of living. We began putting together information about what was possible to achieve in our community, what was possible where we lived. But more than this, we spoke from the heart about what we believed in, what our stories had to tell us – the good, the bad, and the ugly – what our beliefs were now based on our experiences versus what we might have been taught but hadn't integrated into our lives.

Despite my knack for finding any excuse to avoid the difficult (you should have seen the all ways we found to avoid finally sitting down!), there was a profoundly surprising benefit. Yes, we each know now what we'd prefer, complete with roles and goals, if at all possible. Yes, it was emotional. Yes, it was honest. But what I didn't expect was that it was oddly, bizarrely liberating.

Yes. Liberating.

Once the clouds parted from the shock of having honestly talked about our own impending mortality, a burden lifted that I hadn't even realized I was carrying: the ultimate fear, not of death itself, but of denying the reality of it by not speaking about what will happen to me.

If you've ever been forced to keep a secret, whether for your own or another's protection or from fear of what might happen if you spoke the truth, you understand what I'm talking about. Your life energy appears full to others on the outside, but a part of you always knows you're living a lie. A part of you is parked behind closed lips or shelved behind a dusty box in some dark cupboard. And when one day, for whatever reason you choose to take that box down off the shelf, the combination of fear and trepidation, followed by the decision to speak the truth – no matter what the outer reaction might be – releases an inordinate amount of potential energy that had been bottled up within you.

In sharing what really mattered to me for the end of my life, I was taking responsibility, as best I could, for what truly mattered to me, amidst the unknowable future. And I felt lifted, lighter, full of a different sort of energy. I didn't realize that on a much deeper level, I was freeing a space within me where I had subconsciously been storing a lie: that I would live forever, that death would never knock at my door.

Though I'd taught this in so many ways over the years and encouraged others to think about this fact, until I had that conversation with the person I loved most in the world about my own death, my care, and my last days on this earth, I had no idea that I was actually a card-carrying member in the club of denial. I was simply masquerading, in full dramatic professional costume, as someone who wasn't.

Truth spoken.

I actually won't be here forever.

And this is where things got interesting.

Of course I knew this, on one level. But really owning it? It was the difference between talking about getting married and signing the certificate. Talking about a vacation, and getting on the plane. It was that different. This, in itself, was a powerful revelation. And one, I might add, not unique to me among those drawn to work with, in, or around end-of-life care.

I had taught what the system calls advance care planning, in one form or another, for years. Healthcare staff do this all the time – teach or ask others what their wishes are. Yet until I made the time to sit down with my partner and explore what really mattered most to each of us, what we believed death was, what we would want, what we would never choose, or what we were still uncertain about, I truly didn't get the reality for myself that the "them" that we were always talking about was me, was us.

Nearly simultaneous with the energy of releasing this internal burden of denial was a surging tidal wave of thoughts that went something like un-ending cycle of this: "$*&^ , I don't have forever. What the #@!> am I doing with my life?"

So as I had my conversation and hit the tough stuff, I realized why, even though I'd taught others the importance of the conversation, I'd put it off myself for so long. I wasn't really afraid of dying. When I took the cover off and looked at it up close and personal, what I really feared was not having lived my life.

That was why, as a healthy Baby Boomer woman, I'd put it off. This was the core of my denial. The belief that somehow if I avoided thinking or talking about my own death, or my fear of my true love dying, I could avoid looking at the real deal – that this life is precious precisely because it is limited. And what was I doing with mine?

Our conversation did what no coaching or self-help book from the past achieved: it helped me define my beliefs and what matters most to me, not just in dying but in living. It opened the door to saying things we might never have said about our beliefs on life and on death, on love, and on letting go.

Through this lens, we each found a new inner compass – and we each received a kick in the pants to get on with living now, not later. While I know we weren't the first to make this connection, it was the first time I felt it in my bones.

This inspiration was the original foundation for both the inner call and the impetus to get on with the vision for my work and my life. It fueled the energy needed to focus, create, and launch Conversations for Life. The staff workshops, the public health campaign, and the community facilitation were all based on the intersection between my personal realizations, my calling, and the very touchable reality that I don't have forever on this earth – and neither does anyone else.

What I learned firsthand was that beyond the impact this conversation can have our how we live our last days, how we choose to face our mortality is an internal and personal process for every one of us. It's not just something we have a conversation about or do for others.

It offers the key to not leaving the spiritual or heart-centered parts of ourselves behind (or reminding ourselves very quickly when we begin to). It offers us a key to truly making a difference in our lives, in our work, with our family, or in our communities. If you're not sure if you're on the right path, it's the key to helping define how you want to live, what you want to do, and how you will define your legacy.

It was the impetus to launch and the reminder, when it began to feel like something was missing. It was also the key to the realization that I was attempting to control an outcome, yet again. To do it by myself. To live up to the Big Kahuna plan I had envisioned for myself – even when I was exhausted and literally dying inside trying to make it work. It reminded me to take a breath. Let go. And consider another way.

It's why I decided to write this book – and now to finally finish it. Because I believe the way forward is up to each of us who are called to make a difference. And if you're still reading this, I believe you are someone who can.

Chapter 9

Life Lessons

Don't be fooled. Though this is a profound chapter title, I'm in this with you as far as the lessons life and death have to teach. Yet what I know from my experiences, without a shadow of a doubt, is this:

- Facing versus denying our experiences of death can empower our life and inform our legacy – by focusing our lives on what matters most now.
- It can also impact how and where we may live our last days in the future – or the care of those we love.
- So our lives and our future care may well depend on what we each do (or choose to not do) between now and then.

Bottom line: most of us don't talk about these things, because it's either for later, for someone else, or we figure, what's the point? In the end, we're all going to die anyway. Yet we all want to make a difference. And this is our life we are talking about.

Just like my mother, we can't possibly have the power to choose to make a difference if we don't know there is a difference we can each make – for ourselves, with our families, and in our communities. We can't possibly summon the courage to choose to begin if we're too busy (or too ensconced in our belief that we'll live forever) to listen to what's true in our hearts. And we can't possibly be inspired to know the difference that can be made if we don't share the stories of what's working.

I know. I've been there.

Once I made the connection, explored and integrated what death was for me – based on my experiences, beliefs, and what mattered most to me for my last days of living – it provided me the clearest road map to what I'd been searching for all along, deeper meaning and focus in my life between now and then, to make the difference I could make, as defined by me, not someone else.

I know I am not unique in this.

The time has come for many of us to honor all we know and have experienced as women and men, families and communities. The time has come to stop putting it off. To become part of a revolution, a transformation of the fear or denial of death and dying into a public-led movement for compassion and care. To reclaim, in the large and small ways available to each of us, our authentic voice, our connection to that still, small place inside that says, "Enough!" or "Why can't it be like this?" To stop looking outside of ourselves for the answers about who we are, what we are here to do, and how we are to care for each other at the end.

We were born knowing the answers.

It is our legacy to live them – and, in the end, to support each other to let go.

So much of what we read and hear is about fear, about forms, about legal battles. And all of these are real. Yet the stories, models and services that are actually available are not connected in a way that holds our collective hand and says, "Here, this is how you do it. This is how you can get what you truly want for your last days of living." The only ones who know those stories are those who've lived them.

No person or community or system is the same. And no one person holds the answer for you. But by joining together and sharing our stories of what works, we might just realize we're not alone. We connect from the heart – and that is where the motivation to make a difference comes from.

So If you're someone who thinks the best way to go is to die suddenly, or in your sleep, understand this: statistically, fewer than 10% of us will die suddenly. And if you do ask those whose mothers, sisters, fathers, or brothers died suddenly what they most regret, it's that they couldn't say goodbye, couldn't share unspoken words of love and wisdom.

Where the hell were any of those loved ones' life's details? What in heaven's name would they have wanted for their funeral? Where was the paperwork, the house deed, and the banking records, and why did it take longer to sort all of this out than it did for them to leave this earth?

If you are very religious or spiritual, you may well have come to peace with death. Yet even with that belief, many find themselves utterly unprepared for the maze of decisions and realities around healthcare, social care, legal forms, and realities that make up dying in the 21st century. Our beliefs and values can bump up against the realities faced by even the most caring staff working in institutions, many of whom are ill-equipped themselves to accept the reality of mortality.

One man in his thirties told me his family was very religious before his father's death. After his father's friend, a surgeon, came out of the operating room to tell the family that he "didn't make it," he shook his head and said the doctors had not actually thought surgery would save his life, but it was all they could do. The family was left feeling enraged that their last days with their father and husband were stolen from them. After the death, they left the church and had serious questions about their faith.

If you are highly scientific, left-brained, or firmly medically-based, realize that there are many who find themselves completely taken aback at the bedside of the dying when something "spiritual" happens that medicine or science hasn't prepared them for. King's College in London surveyed staff working with dying patients in hospices and found common end-of-life experiences including events characterized as "transpersonal," "mystical," and "spooky." As one nurse in a workshop told me, "I've thought a lot about what death means, but this workshop has created connections between many experiences I've had with others' deaths that never quite made sense. This has been a gift."

What I learned from my experiences around my mother's death is that death is more than physical. No one approach, in and of itself – not just a conversation, not simply a form, not the spiritual beliefs nor the understanding of the medical system – provided the solution we wanted. It was experiencing all of them together, the combination of information, skills, and resources that needed to come together where we lived, to achieve what we needed during the only event that is certain for all of us. Nothing had prepared us for this.

So what can we do?

I am one woman with a story. I have done and continue to do what I know how to make a little ripple in that Big Kahuna plan. Yet what have I learned since sitting on that beach in Maui years ago is that this campaign, this culture change, this movement to reclaim death as a natural part of life, to create compassionate communities, to bring our loved one's home if that's what they choose, is quite literally up to all of us.

To really make an impact, more people need to know that they, too, can make a difference – that their stories and experiences can inspire them, like mine did, to do something about it. For you to know this in your bones. That all of us equals each of us. For your life. About your death. And with your legacy.

And to know you are not alone. By coming together, we are leading the way.

From the thousands I've met now in workshops and conferences internationally, the stories, the staff and the projects I've been involved in, I now know without a doubt that there are people in every community who have gifts and skills to share that can make a difference: neighbors with knowledge or the gift of cooking a meal, those who can drive you to an appointment or sit beside you, healthcare staff doing amazing jobs in insane circumstances, current and retired nurses and social workers, counselors and caregivers from faith groups, and those who are called to teach or facilitate how to start conversations. It all already exists, alongside the compassionate staff and the medical systems they may work for.

Yet they need us to become informed. To share and learn from what works. To speak up.

And we need them to heed the call, as well. To truly make the difference they are here to make.

"No transformation in medicine has ever come from within medicine."

That quote rang in my head after I heard a geriatrician say it at an international conference I recently attended.

If we await a system-led or system-wide solution to incorporate these ideas into a care package, we will wait a long time, at best. Not to mention that these gifts will be compressed into a box that can be tracked by a project manager and calculated on a form. It's what systems do.

Life and death don't fit on a form. And research now proves we live fuller lives when we share our compassion and gifts with others.

It is up to all of us to bridge the gaps by working together in simple yet powerful ways. All of us are human, those in board rooms and operating rooms no less than those in bedrooms and community meeting rooms. All of us will need the care we create together, between now and an unknown then. What I've learned is that both head and heart are needed.

Why now?

Here's the raw truth.

Systems have compartmentalized information and approaches to the point of making the natural process of dying inaccessible to those caring for the dying and incomprehensible to those going through it.

There is no form. There is no one person. There is no one way.

Medicine has no cure for mortality.

Death is certain.

And death is more than physical.

What I learned was that even though forms exist for good reasons, there is no form that creates compassionate care.

Even though conversations offer a key, professionals, family members, and adult children find ways to avoid them. There are tools that can help, but there is no script.

Even though we all will one day breathe our last breath, there is no one way; there will only be your way.

What I learned from my story and my experiences is also supported by the larger picture:

- Most Americans expect their families to carry out their wishes about end of life care, yet 75% admit they have never clearly articulated what those wishes are, and their children are afraid to ask.
- 80% of people surveyed would prefer to live their last days at home with support, while, in reality, 70-80% are living their last days in institutions.
- Although the public expect (and would trust) their doctors to have these conversations with them, 40% of doctors have never had this conversation with their own family members.
- Most doctors, when given the chance, choose to limit medical interventions for their own last days, just as my mother did.
- Doctors are humans and, as such, are no better equipped to face mortality than the rest of us. Research shows that their estimates for how long someone has left to live are often overstated. "One week before death, the average patient still had a 40% chance of living six months," according to a landmark study on the accuracy

of doctors' prognoses by Dr. Joanne Lynn. ("She has three weeks!" "Really, that long?" Um ... no.)

- Forms are required by systems to communicate what we want when we can't speak for ourselves. Great. Yet even the best form has a human being at the end of it required to interpret it, act upon it, or choose. We really don't want healthcare staff who cannot think for themselves, but at the same time there isn't a human alive who knows what's best for us at every moment of our lives. We have to translate what matters to us into the forms – which is their language – while ensuring that others in our circle of support can speak up for us if needed.

- A recent study in Australia described the "best" end-of-life care: in 128 days of patient care, the time of staff or professional visits totaled 24 hours. One day. That leaves 127 days counting on the love, compassion, and brass-tacks care of family and friends. Community is required to create a culture of care.

- A similar study that gathered families who'd cared for a loved one at home for their last days, has shown that they expanded their support networks as a result (not become more isolated, as the media suggest), and after their experiences were now more "death literate," with greater awareness, information, and commitment to making a difference as a result.

Unless we educate ourselves about the end of life, become "death literate," and speak about what matters most to us, we will become another statistic – and we may just miss the greatest opportunity death gives us: to focus our life on what matters most between now and then.

So if you can relate, if the death of someone you loved resonates with the statistics above, if you know you would never want or choose the care that they received, or if you, like me, have a story of what worked, what supported someone you loved to get the care for the last days that they chose, please know you are not alone. Please do something about it.

Share your story – and start your conversations.

Our stories inspire us to make a difference.

And our desire to make a difference is not ours alone.

What I now know is that my vision is one of many.

This is a movement, and the movement has already begun.

People who are dying to make a difference are coming together internationally. Thousands of incredible people and organizations are working around the world to make this a reality in our lifetime.

New national campaigns to start the conversation exist internationally; initiatives and approaches from within and without healthcare systems are shifting toward more compassionate care.

Pilot projects, charities, and community groups are finding ways to make connections and create compassionate communities, while supporting death literacy, home funerals, and conscious, mindful care.

Baby Boomers are planning new ways to live their last days with meaning and in community. All of this is fantastic forward movement. All of it needs our support. And we can all play our roles in making a difference, if we choose.

It's up to us.

How this story ends is up to us.

Chapter 10

Choosing Freedom

Don't let me fool you. Even though I have seen death up close and personal, even though I have worked in end-of-life care, it has taken a while to sink in that I will one day die.

But by getting beyond the seeming morbidity of this fact and getting past being pissed off, I finally saw that the gift of this simple truth was not limitation or fear. It was freedom.

My mother's choice was to accept her death, full-on and facing forward.

My mother's gift was to offer me this choice, too – to accept all of it and live life with death. Not either/or. Both/and.

Following my mother's death, I was consumed with the power that information and choices gave us – as if we ultimately had some control. Yet the ultimate power to choose was not having a choice of life or death – or the power with or over medical or legal establishments, or policies or institutions.

The ultimate power is the power that's possible when we individually and collectively stop denying the one true fact: this lifetime is inherently limited. For every one of us. And if we choose to orient our lives around this truth, we gain access to the ultimate power to accept both/and – medicine and spirituality; system and community; mind, body and spirit; head and heart; love and letting go: life and death. In short, freedom.

And this shift in perception can also influence our future care.

How we as individuals, families, and communities accept or deny this fact influences far more than our care at the end of life (as if that isn't enough). It impacts the way we choose to live. It gives us real freedom: to choose what matters, what we believe in, who or what we give power to, what we're going to say no to and yes to – and how we might just take a stand we would never have taken before or allow our hearts and minds to open unexpectedly. How we are all in the same boat, no matter what color or creed, who we love, how many letters come after our name or how little money is in our pockets. How nothing material can define the worth of another human being. The ultimate dance of life, with death as our partner, is one we are all in together. Not either/or. Both/and.

The doctor that sits before you. The educator that teaches the course. The neighbor next door. The colleague at work. Your best friend or lover. Your worst enemy or challenger. Your faith or tradition. Their faith or tradition. Every single one of us will one day die. And in this commonality, there is one way in (birth) and one way out (death). What we do with the middle is up to us to create. We have no control over the quantity of our life, but in each moment we can choose its quality.

Imagine if we were all taught this as children. Imagine if those entering medical or nursing school were given a course in the natural cycles of life and death, the impact of belief, the wisdom from other cultures. Imagine if our faith or religion allowed for a discourse around the nuts and bolts of care of the dying. Imagine if we all understood that death wasn't a failure to be feared, but a process, an experience that we could gain wisdom about and create support for, as we do birth. Imagine.

It takes only a glimpse at cultures and practices that respect death as part of the natural cycle of life to see the ripple effect of such beliefs: honoring versus institutionalizing the elderly, caring for versus pillaging of the earth, and the sustainability of aligning community wisdom with nature versus against it. Perhaps when we listen to and learn the wisdom of other cultures, combined with the best medicine that technology has to offer, we will free our hearts and minds to unite in what really matters, creating communities that care not only for the dying (which includes all of us) but for the living as well. Perhaps those who care and the systems they work for would not then need to leave their human self behind in the name of care.

"If the walls came down between us, we could reach and care for everyone in our community."

Years later, those words still ring in my ears.

No small thing, our image of what death is.

No small thing, the beliefs we hold about it.

No small thing, what is possible when we know we can make a difference.

If you have ever been privileged enough to sit at the bedside of someone who was taking their last breaths, you may have witnessed something extraordinary that informed your life. Through even the most debilitating illnesses, there is often a light, a brightness, that shines through as the end is coming near. Call it consciousness or soul or spirit – whatever language you will.

For me, I've come to accept that birth is a soul's entering the form of a body and death, a soul leaving that form. The connection between both, the eternal element, is the consciousness, light, spirit, or soul that has come into this world to make a difference in the unique ways it can. And in that space, what we are here to learn about is love.

Whenever we connect to that place within, we are being our most authentic selves. When you speak with a child, or someone who is dying, there is a directness, an authenticity, a clarity. It is our essential nature. It is what many of us long for, strive to achieve in our life, and it is what has been there all along. Some realize this in death, and they are blessed. To realize this in life is a gift worth more than gold.

What I've uncovered within my own story is that my mission is not about a conversation or about death and dying at all. It is about life and living. Really living. About love and letting go. About remembering the precious and inherent nature of life's cycles working within each of us, and the profound influence we can each have in the lives (and deaths) of those around us – and, if we are most fortunate, the profound influence that they will have in ours.

So the surprising reason I remain passionate about the end of life is that it offers a daily reminder of the precious time we have to bring what we know, love, and believe in to make our difference now. To follow our inner voice. To slow down. To listen. To be present to the things that really matter.

They say you teach what you most need to learn…

Point well taken.

Clearly I am a slow learner!

Yet when I do this, when I listen, it makes a difference. When I slowed down to listen to my mother, I had one of the most profound conversations of our life. When I slowed down and made the time to talk with my love about what we wanted for our end-of-life care, I learned more about the unique and soulful connection between us, about things we'd never spoken to another human being, more than we'd learned in four years overcoming the challenges of international relationships, immigration, and driving on the wrong side of the road.

After making the time with my sister and brother-in-law to share together what we'd want and never choose for our future care, do you know what we ended up talking about? Other than key information, like medical intervention or natural dying or spirituality?

What we ended up talking about was the same thing that guided and carried us through my mother's death: love. I learned more about my sister and brother-in-law's love for each other in one hour than I had in 18 years of knowing them together.

And in a poignant, hilarious exchange in one of my first Conversations for Life workshops, one of two daughters whose mother had been diagnosed with cancer said: "It's like when you finally fix up everything in your house just before you go to sell it. And then you wonder why it was only then that you allowed yourself to have it how you would have liked it all along. I learned things about my mother today that I never would have known if we hadn't had this conversation before she died."

After her mother died months later, I got an email thanking me for the difference the workshop made to them all.

Why do we wait?

When I slow down and listen, to those I love most or to my inner voice, I create the opportunity to connect to what matters most. And from there, I – and we – can truly make a difference.

When I get off track, knocked off balance, start getting into my head or the "How's it going to work?" questions that my nagging brain likes to incessantly sing, I remember.

This is my life.

I have choices.

And I ask: is what I'm now doing aligned with what matters most to me or have I veered off course?

What else are we missing in the whirring busyness we call living? It took a conversation about death to call my mother and me to speak from our hearts. It wasn't a conversation for death, it was a conversation for life, literally a conversation that helped her achieve what she wanted most for what turned out to be her final days of living. A conversation that ultimately helped me create a map of what really mattered for my life. Somehow the richness of living gets enhanced through really accepting the fact that we will one day die.

And when I really, deeply listened to what I was saying about my beliefs and values, about the God I knew personally and the things that mattered most for my future care, what I heard myself saying was what mattered to that deepest place within me, that still small voice. That place that we give precious little time to but has been there all along.

What I touched and had the opportunity to listen to was my soul.

From that place I held:

- The freedom to choose to accept what I believe today, not what I was taught or learned or told I should believe or do. To hear and integrate my own limiting beliefs, like

"God's will, not mine," which my mother carried without clarifying what that meant to her as time went on.

- To choose to not wait for my death to let go of the beliefs I no longer value and step more fully into a life defined by what I truly believe. If what I choose is aligned with my soul's purpose, then doors will open more easily. If not, I can notice that, course-correct and choose again.

- The freedom to define what making a difference means to me. Not to my head or ego, or to what others think I should or could do next, but from my heart. In grand sweeping brushstrokes, like packing up and moving to another country, or in the simple choice to rise an hour earlier to slow down and savor a cup of tea. To be OK with myself – with what I do or say, even if it isn't perfect – especially when it isn't.

- The freedom to be radically, unapologetically, uniquely me. To allow my life to be an expression of the odd mix of gifts that I am, not just one part. To push the boundaries of what's possible. To hold multiple and oftentimes contradictory information or experiences as simultaneously true. And when I'm faced with an either/or, to allow myself to hold both/and and see what comes from that.

- The freedom to be patient. To allow that I can't possibly know the timing of life any more than I can know the timing of death. To allow myself the compassion that I would offer others: recognizing that life and death are operating at some level in everyone I meet. Although I can make a difference, I am but one of millions each expanding their awareness, actions, and reach. That I don't have to do it all, nor can I. That I am not alone. I am a small part of a greater whole, as is everyone I come in contact with. That real change takes time, so why am I rushing?

- The freedom to not have the answers, but to continue to ask the questions. To get back to not knowing by choice, not by failure. To not accept what is, yet to not throw it out either. To stay curious and remember to enjoy the unexpected things that arise as a result. To recognize that even though I think I want the known, the unknown is where life lives and where I can expand rather than contract into what the future holds for me.

If we are each to leave our own legacy and make the difference we are uniquely here to make, we might just need to be authentically ourselves to do so. And death not only gives us the freedom to be us, but gives us a kick in the pants to get on with it – now.

Chapter 11

Leaving a Legacy

There's a lot of talk these days about leaving a legacy. As I explored the lessons from my own experiences, I remembered that others had shared their soul's insights with me along the way when I asked. And I truly wanted to listen.

Before he died, I had the privilege and opportunity to interview one of the founding fathers of the human potential movement and author of *Mastery*, George Leonard. When I asked him about how he lived with the reality of death, he told me:

"To be honest, I've experienced a lot of death in my life, yet I've not spent much time thinking about it ... I guess the message is, 'Get on with it.'"

He stood up, reached his hand into his back pocket, and pulled out of his wallet a folded, yellowed piece of lined paper, creased with years of being held in his back pocket. It was a remarkable letter his daughter had written to him describing what he taught and meant to her as a father. A simple letter she'd taken the time to write. A letter that had, unexpectedly, outlived her – she died from cancer too young – and that her father cherished forever.

There is so much more love within us than we ever speak or share. If nothing else, let the reality of death grant you permission to share it. Let your experiences show you the wisdom of life as a whole. Let your conversations, your hopes for your future, your vision for what's possible in your family or community, come back to the essential truth for us all: this life is precious precisely because it is limited. And when it all comes down to it, what matters most to us is love.

It's about love.

For what matters most in the end is what mattered most all along, yet we somehow don't believe we have permission or the right to choose to be *that* much or care *that* much or speak up *that* much.

When faced with the reality of those you love one day dying and realizing what you mean to them, life itself takes on an entirely new meaning and gives you a wake-up call. This IS it. This IS your life. You are granted permission. Get on with it.

Precisely what gave my mother the freedom after so many years to speak up about her fears, to say what was true in her heart, to stop making doctors into God, I will never know. I do know that the freedom for me came when I integrated my experiences of death with my beliefs, my hopes, and my desire to make a difference. From a place of love, not fear, death offered me a freedom to choose how I move forward, choose to make a difference, and even leave a legacy myself.

And, yes, when I forget – especially in those times I feel the most stuck or can only see the impossibility of "freedom to choose" – reminders come in the never-ending flow of life-changing moments: the diagnosis of a friend or sudden death of a loved one, stories of what works and what's possible. Reminders that life is short and precious –that I get to choose.

Whatever your beliefs, the pain and grief of loss can last a lifetime. Yet the freedom we each have to choose the lessons we learn and apply in our life as a result, I'm beginning to realize, are death's gift of love that can inspire our desire to make a difference and create a new story, for our life, our future, our legacy.

Living with dying is an ongoing, transformational process. I continue to apply and learn from the lessons death teaches the living, while being passionate about how the living can care for the dying (and fully aware that there is no "us" and "them" in that sentence).

Though raising this awareness started out as an altruistic mission for me, now that I'm over 50 it is becoming self-defense. I continue to unpack and learn from my experiences, focusing my work and my life on what matters most to me. Being guided by my inner compass – that small clear voice within – to reflect and course-correct my life.

What death continues to each me about life is this:

The two are connected.

The courage to choose is required. To look at life and
death facing forward isn't for the faint-hearted. But courage
can emerge in simple acts over time. And it can catch you by
surprise, when and where you least expect it. It can also help
you speak up, and get what you want for your life and your last
days of living.

**The power to choose is only possible when we know
there are choices to be made at all** – when we have the facts
before us and trust our gut to lead us to make the best choices
for our current circumstances now, which can't help but impact
our future. When we don't leave it to someone else, or for some
later time, but take the initiative ourselves. When we come
together in our circles of friends and family or community, as
a collective. When we know we are not alone, it is much easier
to come back to what matters most. To have a team of support
who will listen, who will care – in my life and for my last days.

**The freedom to choose is an internal piece, a deeply
rooted personal permission granted.** There may simply
be a moment when you know it's time: time to believe your
experiences, time to hear your own story for what it has to
teach you – and others. Time to let go of all of the "shoulds" that
no longer serve you. Time to say, "Enough is enough." Time to
think, in this very moment, will this path not taken become a
"woulda, shoulda, coulda" in the future? Time to believe, finally,
you are worth it and just might be able to say what you really
believe and begin anew.

As a dear friend and hospice director says to me often,
"We don't have forever. We have all the time that there is."
Or as Steve Jobs, the founder of Apple Computer, put it in his

commencement address at Stanford University nearing the last days of his own life, "Death is the greatest invention."

Not the iPad, not the internet, not a piece of beautiful technology that adorns millions of laps and desks, into which I myself typed my story though snot bubbles on a plane ride in 2004. Nope.

Death.

The greatest invention.

So, yes. Get on with it.

Not just your Big Kahuna or to-do list in your life, but the discovery and expression of the unique calling and combination of skills and gifts, of stories and connections, of letters written or yet to write that each of us holds within us without realizing until death knocks the door down or swings it wide open how significant it is. How significant you are. How significant we are to each other.

Your legacy may be to move mountains.

Your legacy may just be being you.

What I didn't realize on that ordinary day in October, in a conversation with my mother on a chintz sofa at Silverdale Grove, was that a simple conversation can provide a catalyst to change your life.

Beyond supporting her wishes for her last days, it changed not only how I may live my own last days but all the days between now and then. In what turned out to be the last ten days of her life, my mother chose. My mother's last gift to me, her daughter, was the absolute freedom to choose.

In the years since my mother's death, I've been astoundingly privileged to hear the stories of, learn from, and work with literally thousands of healthcare staff and members of the public alike. I've facilitated dozens of communities, with leaders and organizations who each wanted to launch their own initiatives to start conversations or connect up strengths in their communities to care. I've been inspired by meeting leaders of international campaigns and wildly innovative projects.

In that time I've lived my life between two communities: the rapid pace of the San Francisco Bay Area and a small village in the north of England where there are as many sheep as people – where, I have to admit, I've learned the benefits of a slower pace and the sheer magic of a cup of tea.

As a Bay Area Baby Boomer living abroad, I have found fantastic information and resources available about starting conversations and caring for people at the end of life that didn't exist when my mother died.

Yet, what I've learned living in a small community is that the Internet won't hold your hand when you need it most. Human hearts and human hands created a world wide web long before the Internet was invented. If we are to create communities that care for all of our days, including our last, we will need to connect, close the gaps, and cross the street. And in the places that this is happening, the term "community" is making a comeback – online and in person. Both/and, not either/or. It's possible, it's happening, and it's the key to creating a more compassionate future for us all.

We are all living in increasingly busy and fast-paced lives. Systems are failing. Change is upon us all. Yet when it all boils down, it makes no difference where you live, what your role is, or how much you have. From rural communities to the inner city, if you're a daughter, a mother, a partner, a sister, or a friend – in the end, we all want the best for our lives and for our last days, for ourselves and for those we love.

We are each mortal.

We all have a story.

Conversations connect.

Care happens in communities.

Every one of us can make a difference.

Together we can make the difference we are here to make.

It might just be our legacy to do so.

What's Next?

You may well be interested in more than I can share in this simple book.

I'd love to learn what matters most to you. What inspirations or questions you have after reading these pages.

To write to me, if you'd like to view the filmed stories mentioned, or learn more about the Conversations for Life approach for Baby Boomers, educators or communities go to www.marymatthiesen.com. I'll update information and blog there as well.

There are literally thousands of places to look for further information or support. You'll find a list in the following pages of some of the individuals and organizations I've been privileged to learn from and work with that may offer you additional information, perspectives or support.

About the Author

Mary Matthiesen
is a partner, a
daughter, a sister, and
a friend.

Her work
coaching individuals
and consulting with
healthcare and
hospice organizations
promotes personal
and collective
culture change in
support of living and
dying well.

She is the creator of Conversations for Life™, a facilitated
approach to engaging communities, staff and families to
address one of the most significant issues facing our generation,
compassionate care for our last days of living.

She holds a degree in psychobiology, was one of the first 50 non-profit leaders in the country to receive a fellowship from Stanford's Executive Non-Profit Leadership program, and is an expert coach/facilitator with certificates from the Asset-Based Community Development Institute, the Cancer Monologue Project, and the Coaches Training Institute.

Mary shares her life, her love, and her time between the US and the UK and works on projects internationally. On a good day, she remembers to listen, ask important questions, and heed life's call. On a not-so-good day, she tries to remember to be compassionate with herself for forgetting.

Resources I Refer People To Almost Daily

Starting meaningful conversations

Conversations for Life, www.conversationsforlife.com

The Conversation Project, www.conversationproject.org

The Four Things That Matter Most: A Book About Living, by Ira Byock

And always, refer to your local hospice and palliative care services to gain the most relevant information for you or your family to be informed in advance of crisis or need: www.nhpco.org (US); www.hospiceuk.org (UK).

Spirituality and Care

Christina Puchalski, MD, George Washington Institute for Spirituality and Health, www.gwish.org

Sacred Dying, by Megory Anderson

The Sacred Dying Foundation, www.sacreddying.org

Graceful Passages (CD), Wisdom of the World Productions, www.wisdomoftheworld.com

Care for the Journey (CD), Companion Arts, www.companionarts.org

The Natural Death Center, www.naturaldeath.org

The Tibetan Book of Living and Dying, Sonyal Rinpoche

Compassionate Community Initiatives

Compassionate Cities & Health Promoting Palliative Care, by Alan Kellehear

The Groundswell Project (Aus), www.groundswell.org

Dying Matters Coalition (UK), www.dyingmatters.org

Public Health and Palliative Care International-Creating Compassionate Communities, www.phpci.org

Abundant Communities, by John McKnight and Peter Block

The Asset Based Community Development Institute, www.abcd.org

And inspirations for living fully and focusing on what matters most

The Desire Map, by Danielle La Porte

Mastery, by George Leonard

Evolving Wisdom Courses, www.evolvingwisdom.com

Printed in Great Britain
by Amazon